The Way of the Traveler

Making Every Trip a Journey of Self-Discovery

Joseph Dispenza

This book is dedicated to Michael Charles Herbert.

Other Books by Joseph Dispenza

On Silence

The Magical Realism of Alyce Frank

Live Better Longer:
  The Parcells Center Seven-Step Plan for Health and Longevity

The Serigraphs of Doug West

Will Shuster: A Santa Fe Legend

The House of Alarcon

Advertising the American Woman

Freeze Frame: A History of the American Film

Re-Runs: Cinema on Television

Forgotten Patriot

The Way of the Traveler

Making Every Trip a Journey of Self-Discovery

Second Edition

Joseph Dispenza

AVALON
TRAVEL

The Way of the Traveler
2nd Edition

Published by Avalon Travel Publishing
1400 65th Street, Suite 250
Emeryville, CA 94608 USA

Distributed by Publishers Group West
Text ©2002 by Avalon Travel Publishing, Inc.
All rights reserved.
Photos are used by permission and are
the property of their original copyright owners.

ISBN: 1-56691-449-3
ISSN: 1539-6436

Please send all comments, corrections,
additions, amendments, and critiques to:

The Way of the Traveler
Avalon Travel Publishing
1400 65th Street, Suite 250
Emeryville, CA 94608, USA

email: atpfeedback@avalonpub.com
website: www.travelmatters.com

Printing History
1st edition—1999
2nd edition—October 2002
5 4 3 2 1

Editor: Rebecca K. Browning
Copy Editor: Emily Lunceford
Production Coordinator: Alvaro Villanueva
Graphics Coordinator: Susan Snyder
Proofreader: Karen Gaynor Bleske
Cover design: Alvaro Villanueva
Cover photos: Top left—©Dugald Bremner; Top right—©Garry Gay/Folio, Inc.;
    Bottom left—©Ulrike Welsh.; Bottom right—©Dennis Johnson/Folio, Inc.
Interior Photos: © Getty Images unless otherwise noted
Illustrations: Laura VanderPloeg

Printed in China through Colorcraft Ltd., Hong Kong

Contents

Part Five: Recounting the Tale

Continuing the Journey

Introduction

There is only one journey. Going inside yourself.

Rainer Maria Rilke

Once you have flown, you will walk the earth with your eyes turned skyward; for there you have been, there you long to return.

Leonardo da Vinci

Racing toward Enlightenment

In 2001, 733 million of us humans were taken off the surface of the planet at one place, transported about six miles into the atmosphere for several hours, then taken back down again at another place. We went willingly, and, for the most part, we enjoyed the experience.

Alien spacecraft did not abduct us. We went in airplanes.

When I first read that statistic from the Federal Aviation Administration—733 million air travelers, more than 12 percent of the human race—I found it difficult to wrap my mind around it. For weeks now I have lived with these figures, and they still surprise me. Even allowing for the fact that one person may have made two or three or a dozen trips in airplanes in that twelve-month period, the number is still staggering—and meaningful.

And there is more: The number of us going up in the sky and coming back down each year in airplanes is projected to rise from three-quarters of a billion in 2000 to 1.2 billion in 2012—that would be around one out of every five of us on the planet. The FAA has predicted that the number of airplane takeoffs and landings will rise from almost 26 million in 2000 to 36 million in 2012, a 39 percent increase—creating traffic jams not in the sky, but on the ground, where the number of runways is far from infinite.

We are traveling in record numbers. Americans alone accounted for nearly 1.1 billion person-trips (one trip taken by one person) in the air, on land, and on the sea last year. Those trips were propelled by 14.4 billion gallons of fuel, at a cost of $7.5 billion. That was national air travel. If you throw in international travel, the bill goes up to over $10 billion—for about 20 billion gallons of fuel. Not only are we traveling more, but we are traveling, it seems, at any cost.

We are also staying away from home for longer periods. In this country, we took an average of seven trips last year, and each trip lasted an average of four days—that adds up to almost a whole month out of the nest for every person in the country.

I find all of this quite encouraging in terms of human evolution. Given that all travel is a journey within, it is heartening that so many of our human family are leaving the comfort zones of home—our present state of awareness—and venturing out into the wild blue yonder: the hidden, yet undiscovered parts of ourselves. Making a journey is always about going from where we are now, to another place, a higher realm of consciousness.

So, as a species we appear to be embarked on a spiritual quest of vast

and unprecedented proportions, searching for the "stranger"—us, undiscovered—at the most profound levels of our individual being.

Once we begin to see travel as an inner journey, it is possible to turn
every trip we take into a spiritual practice—a hero's adventure that enlivens
our hearts and enlarges our souls. Travel becomes a spiritual experience for
us when we are conscious at every moment that our physical transportation
from place to place has a metaphysical counterpart. Understanding that, the
road takes us inexorably to an encounter with the "stranger" at the heart of
the journey—the transformed self.

Undertaken with awareness, travel surely is one of the most available
and most effective means to nourish, broaden, and quicken the soul. The
destination does not matter as much as the attention we give to the understanding that all travel is inner travel.

When we venture out into the world (into ourselves) with that knowledge, we are giving meaning to even the most mundane trip—and giving
ourselves the opportunity to grow our life of the spirit in ways we might
never have imagined.

I believe we do this even if we are not fully awake to it yet. This is why
when I see travel statistics that indicate we are evolving into a race of travelers, it is cause for joy. To me, the numbers mean that our species is flying
back to the Creator with the news of our dawning spiritual awareness—and
we are doing so at supersonic speeds.

*Leaving home in a sense involves a kind of second birth
in which we give birth to ourselves.*

Robert Neelly Bellah, *Habits of the Heart*

The Journey of a Lifetime

Shortly after the first edition of *The Way of the Traveler* appeared, I began
hearing from readers about how they were using the book. I had expected
that mindful travelers would try their hands at some of the activities I suggested in the more practical parts of the book. And I did learn from many
readers that they had enhanced and elevated their travel by creating a travel
shrine, for instance, or by keeping a fear box before a trip, or by packing
spiritual provisions on cards in their overnight bags.

What I had not anticipated was that some readers would take the book
along with them as a guide on inner journeys that were separate and apart
from the physical trips they were making in the world. Packing the book
away in a carry-on case and dipping in and out of it for ideas or inspiration
on a plane was one thing; sitting down in an easy chair with the book and
working through the stages of the hero's journey was quite another.

From experience, I had known that the ancient paradigm of the mythic
quest could be applied to travel with tremendous benefits to the traveler. In my

own travels, I had been doing that for a few years before I wrote the book, and I had felt deeply enriched by it. So much of our travel is done unconsciously. Connecting with mythological archetypes was one way of transforming a mere trip into something really special—a quest for inner knowing. While working on the book, I began to understand that the model of the hero's journey could be relevant to many areas of life besides taking a trip. However, since the focus of *The Way of the Traveler* was on travel, I spoke, I thought, only to that.

But the archetype of the hero's journey itself seemed to have an intention of its own. A few weeks after the book arrived in stores I was receiving letters from readers who thanked me for showing them a new way of putting not just their trips, but their lives, in order. One woman wrote to say that she was finding the book useful as a way of coping with the recent death of her mother. She had found in the ancient structure of the journey an appropriate metaphor for a significant life event—in this case, mourning the loss of a parent—and was following the stages through to the end, in part so that the grieving period actually would come to an end.

Another woman told me that after reading the book she was beginning to see the arc of a relationship that had just ended. Tracing the relationship through the five stages of the hero's journey afforded her the opportunity of understanding how and why the relationship began, how it proceeded—often through challenging circumstances—and how and why it ended. By writing to me about it, she was in the final stage of the paradigm, "recounting the tale," of that bittersweet journey.

A man wrote me with his tale of a journey through a corporate career, from receiving a literal "call to journey" from one of the corporation's headhunters to embroilments in deal-making, financial winning and losing, elation and disappointment, painful office politics, and the rest. Now, at journey's end, he was immeasurably wiser about the ways of the world and about himself. The archetypal structure of the hero's quest allowed him to reflect on that long, important episode in his life and to learn its invaluable lessons.

The book's journey paradigm also found its way into the classroom: a seminar leader read from *The Way of the Traveler* to his photography students, encouraging them to regard their photographic experiences as "a journey of true seeing." By working through the stages of the course from preparation to homecoming, they would arrive at a deeper understanding of their aesthetic encounter.

About the great myths, Carl Jung says, "It is possible to live the fullest life only when we are in harmony with these [mythological] symbols; wisdom is a return to them." The myths had come into these readers' lives, allowing them to find a richer meaning in what they had thought were in-significant or disconnected bits of human living. Travel "out there" is still on most readers' minds, but increasingly the five-stage model of the journey is emerging for many as a tool for personal transformation, whether travel-ing in a car, a train, a plane—or an armchair.

A LifePath

Deeper readings of the book suggested to me that the classical paradigm of travel could be used to raise consciousness in many areas of life. In fact, since life itself is a kind of journey, seeing it as a mythic quest could shed light on some of its mysteries. I was thinking about that when Dr. Beverly Nelson, a psychologist with a long background in holistic healing, contacted me suggesting we collaborate on a *Way of the Traveler* program for people seeking clarity about how they were living their lives.

For three months, we worked on what we called the LifePath Model™, and then we tried it out with a small group of people in a five-day retreat. The results were astonishing. By going through the five stages of the epic journey, our retreatants were able to identify and overcome mental and emotional obstacles that had been preventing them from moving forward in a positive direction with their lives. We were gratified to see people get clear on issues of career, relationship, finances, family history, physical health, self-worth, and more by assuming the role of a hero and venturing through the five archetypal stages. The model was effective beyond our expectations.

With two other colleagues, Beverly and I have been conducting these five-day guided retreats for almost two years now. The scores of retreatants who have gone through the LifePath program continue to report back on the significant changes they were able to make in their lives afterward.

One woman, who had always been pleased pursuing what she considered her true life's work—she was a successful business executive—but had always been unhappy in her personal life, realized that for years she had been repressing a burning desire to be a painter. By the time she completed her hero's journey, she had decided to leave her company for a year to nourish the artist within her and allow that part of her personality to express itself.

An attorney who went through the program discovered just the opposite about his life's work. Unhappy in his career, he had assumed that "the law" was stealing his soul. Actually, it was the unethical attitudes and actions of some of his fellow professionals that had made him depressed and on the verge of abandoning his calling. When he strode through the stages of the journey, he began to see that he could not only continue in his career with a good conscience, but he could also transform the profession by his own sensitivity to ethical issues.

A middle-aged couple went on the mythic journey to save a faltering marriage and found at the heart of their quest a simple truth that they never had gotten around to expressing to one other: "I will not leave you." That was enough to re-create the relationship from the bottom up, this time around mutual trust.

The archetypal framework does most of the transformational work; when sincere seekers engage it to clear up the unfinished business of their lives, magic seems to happen.

Sense of Adventure

However else you decide to use this book, I encourage you to see in the five mythic stages of travel a structure for gaining deeper self-awareness. Certainly it can heighten your physical travel in the world to connect with the ancient paradigm of the journey. But more, it can bring to all that you do, whether physically traveling or not, a sense of epic adventure.

Travel transforms us fundamentally—it must, because it moves us literally from one place (the old) to another (the new). When we have been there for some time and have learned the lessons of that place, travel takes us up to the next level of consciousness, where new insights about ourselves await us.

With our retreats, based on the book, we ask people to leave home and travel to where we are (we are based in Mexico), so they can experience the concept of the mythic journey on both the internal and external levels. Leaving home is essential to understanding the whole of the mystical quest; no hero can return home triumphant if he never leaves home in the first place. Once on the road, we begin to encounter the miraculous.

Travel in the outside world, with all its glorious discoveries, can also transform us within if we become conscious travelers—awake to the possibilities of gaining ever more knowledge of ourselves and the people orbiting our personal world. Entering into the ancient structure of the mythic journey can bring light and meaning to that process, rewarding us in the end with the hero's trophy of the knowledge that brings wisdom.

Let me suggest that when you go on such a journey with this book in hand, you do it with the intention of gaining clarity about an issue in your life that has been pulling at you. Use this as your companion—as the Roman poet Virgil was Dante's companion and guide in the *Inferno*—and see how the archetype of the hero's quest can work for you.

To help, I have expanded each of the five sections of the book with introductions to emphasize the mythological elements of the journey stages. There is more information, also, on the myths themselves, and on the heroes who drive the stories of epic adventure.

In this new edition, you will also find journal prompts that will offer ideas to help start your journaling and note-taking, if you feel moved to do that. Try them out and you will find that your encounter with the ancient hero's journey will be deeper and more practical.

A quick note about the use of the word "hero" in this book: it refers to both women and men. Modern usage of "hero" now includes both genders, according to most dictionaries. I prefer it to "heroine," in any case, because that word seems to suggest, on a subtle level, "less than a hero." From my own experience, witnessing many heroic women perform many heroic deeds, the word "hero" fits both genders aptly and should be applied equally.

Fifty years ago, the great French philosopher and paleontologist Teilhard de Chardin wrote, "We had thought that we were human beings making a spiritual journey; it may be truer to say that we are spiritual beings making a human journey." It is from that perspective that I offer *The Way of the Traveler* to readers in this new edition. When we see all our travels as the movement of our soul ever closer to the light of self-discovery, we are nearing the true destination of all our journeys.

Joseph Dispenza
San Miguel de Allende, Mexico

Once more on my adventure brave and new.

Robert Browning, "Rabbi Ben Ezra"

Starting Out

All travel is inner travel.

A journey is always about going from where we are now to another place. We go literally, but we can also travel figuratively as we search for another, higher level of consciousness.

Seen this way, all our travel has a spiritual character.

And, in this way, all our travel is sacred.

Every time we take a trip, we have an opportunity to expand our awareness and thus to grow spiritually. Travel, undertaken with mindfulness, can be a powerful vehicle for personal transformation.

Whether we are going around the world or merely across town, we can enter the exhilarating adventure of the archetypal, or universal, journey, and we can experience the profound inner metamorphosis that it promises. Conscious travel elevates the process of our journey and enriches our spiritual life.

The literature of all cultures speaks of life as a journey. The great heroes of mythology left the comforts of home and embarked on epic expeditions into the unknown. The accounts of their travels, celebrated in song and passed down through the centuries, form the wisdom of the ages. In myth, the journey of life is an adventure of unparalleled drama and excitement calling forth courage, integrity, generosity, and endurance—and giving back a deep spiritual understanding.

Inspirational literature often refers to the spiritual life as the journey of the soul. The seeker quits the everyday routine and travels inward, into undiscovered country, to find the divine presence at the heart of his or her being. Through meditation, prayer, and other spiritual practices, the searcher for spiritual knowledge makes a pilgrimage to the divinity within—a brave journey requiring the same virtues with which the heroes of myth armed themselves. The end of the journey for both heroes and saints is enlightenment.

If we look at the pattern of the journey as it has come down to us over eons, we see some distinct phases. The first is that of feeling called to journey and imagining how it might be—dreaming about taking the road to another place. Next is preparation: deciding what is to be taken along and what is to remain behind. The third phase involves making the journey itself, with all its serendipitous encounters and amazing unfoldings. After that is the homecoming. And finally, to complete the experience, the traveler recounts the tale of the journey.

This book follows the classical phases of a journey and adds to them a spiritual dimension. It begins with the call to travel. We are restless for movement. We think of leaving where we are and going away, and we imagine what we might encounter on the road to new discoveries.

When the dream of the journey starts to become reality, we actively prepare for the trip. Now a host of choices must be made. What mode of transportation will we use? What belongings need to be packed and brought with us, and what can be left at home? Who will care for what we leave behind?

At last, we embark on the journey itself. The adventures of this trip are amazing, enlarging. We never could have imagined or planned for these people, these sights, these experiences, these openings of the heart.

The journey is over and we return home. But things seem to have changed. In our absence life went on, and we were not a part of it. We are larger, somehow, from our travels, and we see farther. Slowly, all that once was familiar becomes familiar again—but uplifted to something higher.

We close the book of our journey upon the retelling of it. We gather our family, our friends, and show pictures, relate stories, play the music of the place. In this way the journey reaches completion. The lessons learned are passed to those we love.

Travel becomes a spiritual experience when we are conscious at every moment that our physical transportation from place to place has a metaphysical counterpart. Understanding that, the road leads us inexorably to an encounter with the "stranger" at the heart of the journey—we meet ourselves, transformed.

This is the way of the traveler.

I have written this book as a collection of reflections on the spiritual aspects of travel. Each reflection is followed by a simple activity that brings that aspect to life, then by a meditation, or affirmation, to help you seal the thought and make it yours.

The activities in the book are only suggestions—you may come up with your own ways to animate the reflections I have provided. But I highly recommend that you add as many mindful activities as possible to your travel experience. Even small actions of a spiritual nature, you will find, can elevate your travel and bring to it the richness of a sacred event.

In the Middle Ages, pilgrims undertaking a long journey to an important hallowed shrine were given a book of prayers and reflections for spiritual support on the road. The small book was called a *vade mecum*—literally, in Latin, "go with me." Chaucer's Canterbury pilgrims carried these little volumes to strengthen their resolve as they made their progress through the countryside. Don Quixote kept one in his tunic when he ventured out, lance in hand, onto the Spanish plains. Joan of Arc tucked one under her armor, close to her heart, as she galloped into battle.

This book is meant to be that for you—a store of spiritual provisions for your journey in the outer world, which is the road, finally, to self-discovery.

I hope this will be your *vade mecum*.

Putting Your Feelings in Words

You can try this out right now to see how it works. Put a marker in this book and set it aside. Then take out your journal. If you do not have a journal yet, then just a notebook or even a piece of paper will do.

Check in with yourself. How are you feeling? Not what are you thinking, but how are you feeling?

You may be feeling mellow from sitting and reading—or you may be feeling irritable, or frustrated, or sad, or elated, or hopeful. You even may be feeling unclear about exactly how and what you are feeling, or you might be experiencing several different emotions.

Record your feelings. Let the words flow without paying attention to grammar, punctuation, or style—just put your hand on automatic, and let it be the instrument to externalize what is happening in your heart. Write freely. Watch the words appear on paper. Then, when you step back from the page for a moment, try to trace back what might have caused the dominant feeling you have been writing about. If you are feeling irritable, maybe it is because your morning did not go as planned—there might have been interruptions or schedule changes. If you are feeling hopeful, it may be because you received a call from a loving friend, or you were flooded with several new creative ideas. Next to your feelings, jot down what you think might have brought them up.

Now you are doing soul-work. You are making yourself fully conscious and self-aware in the moment.

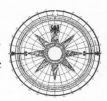

Take only memories. Leave nothing but footprints.
Chief Seattle

A Journal of the Heart

Keeping a journal while on the road is a time-honored tradition. Some of the world's most famous travel books are journals kept by observant and articulate travelers. Many of them are deeply personal records of visiting exotic places. The more personal the journals, the more of "the spirit of the place" they offer us.

As you begin to move toward your own expedition of discovery, consider keeping a journal. But instead of a simple "today I did this, tomorrow I will see that" kind of journal, think in terms of drafting a journal of your feelings.

A journal of feelings is a record of how you felt about the people and things you encountered along the path of your journey.

You might want to begin each entry with, "Today I am feeling. . ."

Committing to paper the vast inventory of emotions you experience during travel serves several purposes. First, it allows you to identify and anchor your feelings. Were you angry at something or someone—elated at a turn of events? Emotions come swiftly when you are away from home and exploring new worlds. Without a way of describing them clearly, gathering them together, and fixing them, they will be lost to the winds.

Next, keeping a journal of feelings makes your trip profoundly more personal. It is one thing to experience a new place in a standard travel brochure way and quite another to be able to react emotionally to it in your own unique manner. The Coliseum? Not just a picture on a poster. You could hear the roar of hungry lions, the clanging swords of gladiators, the thunderous cheers of the crowd; it sent a chill of excitement through you.

Finally, a journal of feelings elevates your trip from a mere sight-seeing excursion to an archetypal hero's journey. Keeping a chronicle of your feelings gives you the opportunity to trace the movements of your heart as you make your way. It transforms a trip of discovery into a journey of self-discovery.

You will find included here occasional prompts to help you start writing in your journal. They suggest themes to get your pen going. Some of them are writing exercises, others ask you to list personal ideas and reflections on the text. Some encourage you to draw or to make collages. All the prompts are designed to deepen your perception of your journey as a rich inner experience.

Part One

The Call to Journey

*Beyond the East the sunrise,
beyond the West the sea.
And East and West the wander-thirst
that will not let me be.*

Gerald Gould, *Wander-Thirst*

When the whistle blew and the call stretched thin across the night,
one had to believe that any journey could be sweet to the soul.

Charles Turner, *The Celebrant*

In myth, epic literature, and sacred traditions, the call to journey comes to the hero at an important turning point in life. When the hero answers the call, huge changes are set in motion—changes that will benefit not only the hero, but also many others and, in some cases, all of humankind.

The call comes, in most stories, just as the hero is about to enter adulthood, and is, in fact, the initiation into that period of life. Perseus, on the brink of manhood, sets out on a journey to win the approval of the man who will marry his mother. Theseus, also approaching maturity, feels called to service by the sight of youths and maidens being taken to Crete as prisoners to be fed to the Minotaur. "When he was fully grown," in the words of historian Edith Hamilton, Jason is called to claim the kingdom from his wicked cousin.

Jesus hears the call to a public life of spiritual teaching at age thirty, and retires to the desert to confront the devil tempter and prepare himself for the great undertaking. At forty, the trader Muhammad is visited by the angel Gabriel, who instructs him in the ways of a prophet, and tells him to go to his people and reveal to them how human beings should live.

For the spiritual philosopher Shankara, the call comes much earlier, at the tender age of eight: while he is bathing in the Puma River, a crocodile catches hold of his leg and will not let it go until the boy's mother, Aryamba, agrees to allow her son to follow the path of an itinerant monk.

Siddhattha Gotama, completing his twenty-ninth year in the splendid palace his father built for him, feels the irresistible pull of the call. Within the walls of the palace grounds, with its many parks and pavilions, Siddhattha's life is idyllic. But when he peers over the walls and sees what his father has always managed to keep from him—in turn, a poor person, a sick person, a corpse, and a monk—he yearns to leave home and seek the "more" that is out in the world.

Whenever and however the call comes, whether through an angel or a devil or a crocodile, the hero's affirmative response to it shakes earth and heaven and creates a whole new universe of possibilities for humanity. Agreeing to undertake the journey expands space and changes history. On a personal level, it elevates the hero to a super-human status: Jesus becomes the Christ, Siddhattha Gotama becomes the Buddha.

The call to journey is the insistent, irresistible pull of our Higher Selves, inviting us to go to the next step, to rise to the next level of ourselves. It may come to us in a thousand different ways. Sometimes it is a literal call to make a trip somewhere. Sometimes the call is subtler, such as an "accidental" meeting with someone who presents us with a new way of seeing the world and ourselves. It may come in the form of a physical or emotional crisis. We use the term "wake-up call" to describe a sudden summons to stop living with illusions, to take better care of ourselves, or to alter our behavior in some basic way.

The call may be something as fundamental as the abrupt realization that certain areas of our lives have become intolerable. Change is needed; our survival depends on it.

Our call to embark upon the journey of higher self-awareness may not be as dramatic as the calls that came to the heroes and spiritual leaders of old, but our reply to it is just as significant. If we ignore the call, we stay where we are, at home. Eventually, a dryness of spirit sets in, then a kind of decay and a gradual drifting away. But if we heed the call and agree to go off on the quest for the new, everything around us seems to fall into place, offering assistance. In the myths, the moment the hero says yes to the call to journey, the gods offer supernatural support.

The call to journey carries within it the shining promise of the entire adventure, from beginning to end. Without the call, there can be no movement at all and no promise of transformation into the higher realms. When it does come, however, and we agree to accept its sacred invitation to go boldly to the uncharted places within, everything shifts.

The whole world holds its breath in anticipation.

Nothing happens unless first a dream.
Carl Sandburg

The Dream of the Journey

The urge to travel starts as a far-off yearning to change where we are. We can somehow sense it, the call of the unconscious to move into the outer world. Listening to the call of that still, small voice deep within is the first step of the journey.

Our journey is born in a kind of sacred restlessness.

In his poem "The Explorer," Rudyard Kipling calls the first dreamy inkling of the journey "a voice, as bad as Conscience" that repeats its message night and day: "Something hidden . . . go and find it."

World literature is filled with references to heroes dreaming about journeys before actually embarking on them. Usually a god or goddess appears in a dream and discloses the news that a journey will take place.

The hero's first reaction is often disbelief, followed by apprehension, "Since I had not planned to make a change, how is this to be?" and then, inevitably, "Wait, I cannot go . . . I am afraid to go." The deity calms the hero with a profusion of assurances and promises to be present invisibly to offer guidance, protection, and solace throughout the trip.

Spiritual texts of all cultures also abound with dreams about journeys. An angel may appear to a sleeping person, announcing the idea of travel. Again, the supernatural being is met with incredulity and uneasiness. And again the person is assured that the journey will be all for the good and that every need along the way will be met with heavenly sustenance.

These illustrations from classical antiquity and from spiritual tradition are not lost on us as we, too, dream about a journey.

Sometimes our dream is just a feeling as we go about our regular routine, a vague discomfort with where we are right now. At other times, it may take a more dramatic appearance. A gentle, otherworldly presence may make itself felt while we sleep or when we are drifting in that hazy territory between sleep and wakefulness.

And the message we receive from that presence is, "Come, depart from this place for a time—the world out there awaits you."

The symbolism of the dream is rich and powerful. It tells us that we can stay here and continue to sleepwalk through our usual paces at home or we can entertain the idea of travel, and with it the possibility of change. It also informs us that if we do answer the call to disengage ourselves from "this place," we will be guided and protected on the way.

The dream of travel announces that each of us has the power to transform our lives in a fundamental way.

And it promises that if we pluck up our courage and agree to undertake the journey, the road upon which we travel will lead to self-discovery.

It is no small promise.

In the dream lies the seed of the entire journey. Just as a seed of a tree contains the entire tree and all of its fruit, the dream of travel has within it the whole arc of our trip—from our leave-taking to our homecoming, and everything in between.

No trip is insignificant, the dream seems to tell us. Every time we leave home and go to another place, we open up the possibility of having something wonderful happen to us.

The dream speaks to us, and what it says is this: When we move out of the familiar here and now, we set in motion a series of events that, taken together, bring about changes at the very root of our beings.

And it is time to change.

From One Place to Another

A friend told me about what she does whenever she feels the impulse, however slight, to travel. It is really the simplest thing in the world, and, like most simple things, remarkably meaningful.

When she feels the call to journey, she consciously moves from one spot to another. That is all! She stands in one place in one room of her house and mentally calls that "home." Then she walks slowly and carefully into another room—to a spot that she has designated "the destination."

To complete the exercise, she walks, just as slowly and carefully, back to her original spot. What could be more elementary than that? And yet, the act of moving from one place to another—from "home" to "destination"—is a microcosmic rendering of the entire journey. It changes your perspective on the world in a fundamental way: things look different from one place to another, and also along the way to and from those places. Doing this activity with mindfulness is tantamount to taking the trip, at least in symbolic terms.

Try this exercise yourself. Moving from one place to another in your home, or from a room of your home to a place outdoors and back again, communicates to your unconscious that you are willing and ready to engage the dream of the journey. For grounding, and to feel the process of the journey fully in your body, try doing this exercise barefooted. By making the effort to physically move in the outside world, you say to the universe and to yourself, "I hear—I accept."

I have heard the distant call of the journey. In a dream,
I have sensed the possibility of personal transformation. Now I
open myself to the dream's suggestion and to its promise.
I allow the idea of the journey to move in me.

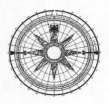

*A good traveler is one who does not know where he is going to,
and a perfect traveler is one who does not know where he came from.*

Lin Yu-t'ang

Where in the World

The world outside is a big place. The world within is even larger. We heed the call of the voice in the dream of travel. We agree to undertake the journey, wherever the road may lead. Now we wonder where we will go.

The most important feature of this phase of the journey is our willingness to engage the call to travel. Seeds have been presented to us in a dream, and we have planted them. Soon shoots will break forth. We will be on the road and, eventually, gathering the fruit of our labors.

Not having been provided a destination, we reflect on where we will go. We ask ourselves what corner of the world is calling us. Where do we feel drawn? Where is the perfect place? Where will the soul find fulfillment?

Not knowing our destination is good. We feel a sense of exhilaration about all the possibilities.

"A good traveler has no fixed plans," says the ancient Chinese philosopher Lao-tzu, "and is not intent on arriving."

While we hear and acknowledge his sage counsel, we also know that we live in a world quite different from his—China of the sixth century B.C. Our world is one in which we need to arrange for airline tickets, to reserve hotel rooms, to check the schedules for ferry crossings, to make plans for auto rentals. It may sound hopelessly mundane, but we do live in the here and now—not in some distant romantic past—and we are subject to the conventions of our time.

Still, at this stage in our journey of self-discovery, we have the great luxury to abide in that special emotional territory to which Lao-tzu guides us—the place of having "no fixed plans." Travel, to be truly conscious, should be a process of gathering knowledge about ourselves. Planning too carefully for that can be counterproductive, and even knowing when we have arrived can be limiting.

So we think about where in the world we want to go. We allow ourselves to feel pulled inexorably to a place. We weigh the prospects, consider the alternatives, entertain the possibilities.

Will this be a new place or a place we have visited before?

Will this journey be an opportunity for a totally new experience against the backdrop of a fresh locale, an exotic, unfamiliar geography—or will it be a place that lingers in the memory and to which we always have been drawn to return, this time with new, different eyes and with more seasoned attitudes?

The destination is still shrouded in the clouds, but our journey has begun.

Set the World Turning

You hear that unmistakable call to make a journey, but you are not given a destination. What next? A number of small things can help you decide where to go.

These activities are reminiscent of childhood games. Perhaps that is why I like them so much. This phase of travel really is—or should be—childlike. With a strong urge to make a trip, but without a specific place to go, we are like children inventing our own play.

Spin-the-globe is one of my favorite pre-travel exercises. It has to be as old as globes themselves. Simply set the world turning and, without looking, put a finger down where it stops. That place becomes a possible destination.

Dream Destinations

Stop for a moment. Think about this: you have the power to create your world anew. You can go wherever you want to go in the entire world. You have just been handed an envelope stuffed with tickets and money. Where will you go? Take the time to write down some of your dream destinations—and how being in those places would deepen your experience of living. Where is your soul drawn? Why?

"I have always wanted to travel to this place, because . . ."

A few years ago when I was feeling the tug to leave home, but I did not know where to go, I played the globe game. Three times, my finger landed in the middle of the Pacific Ocean. I needed to be near water, maybe even in water. I was drawn to a tiny fishing village on the Pacific coast of Mexico. There, alone among the palm trees and the wide vistas of the sea, I received some remarkable insights about my life's direction. The experience near and in water turned out to be life-changing for me. My globe game had been a success.

A similar game is flipping at random through a world atlas. Close your eyes, leaf through the pages slowly, and where you stop becomes another potential place to go.

Still another is lazily perusing a travel magazine or a *National Geographic*. Allow the pictures to draw you in. If an image excites you, let your mind drift as far as it will go into that locale. See yourself there, enjoying the sights, savoring the foods, speaking with the people, and delving into its history . . . and its special mysteries.

The best part of these games is this basic rule: while you do not have to go to these places, you do have to find out one or two facts that you never knew about them. For instance, the mountain range that separates Argentina and Chile is named Tupungato—or in Turkey, one is likely to hear at least six different languages, all of which, together, are called "Turkic"—or in Great Britain, the highest officer of state is neither the monarch nor the prime minister, but the lord high chancellor.

Taking these morsels of information away from pre-travel games can be remarkably helpful as you seek a destination.

Most of the time, your final travel plans have absolutely nothing to do with the exotic lands indicated by your errant fingertip. But the process of physically searching out a place and bringing something back can enhance a journey immeasurably. Wherever you decide to go, these games render the trip a vastly more conscious experience.

I go to where I am called. To discover this destination, I listen deep within. There, in that sacred place, the destination resides. There the journey to self-knowledge is already revealing itself to me.

I am not born for one corner; the whole world is my native land.
Lucius Annaeus Seneca

The Meaning of the Place

Sometimes we feel the pull of the journey, but we do not know what our destination will be. We go within, we listen, we wait. In time, the map of our journey emerges from the mists.

Other journeys are handed to us fully formed and thoroughly charted. As before, we are beckoned forth by the journey, but this time the summons comes to us from the outside. We are called to a wedding, or to a class re-union, or to the bedside of an ailing loved one. Perhaps business takes us to another city, or faraway family members invite us to a holiday gathering.

The destinations of these journeys are already chosen by fate. We know exactly where the trip will take us, but we wonder what will happen along the way, and how we might be transformed by the experience.

All travel is inner travel. Though we did not consciously single out this location, our trip is still very much a journey of self-discovery and personal transformation. Only now we need to discover for ourselves why we might have been called to this particular place over any other.

Since no journey is a mistake, every journey matters.

In the days remaining until we leave home, we ponder the significance of the call to travel, and we try to learn the meaning of the place. If we miss the meaning, we may lose a unique opportunity for growth and self-unfolding.

In a way, we do choose the destination for every journey—but sometimes it appears that we have been drawn to the destination from the outside.

Perhaps we decide on some level of the unconscious that it is time for us to embark upon a journey of self-discovery. What we had believed was a business associate or a family member or a friend is actually our own voice—our deep, unconscious self—drawing us forth to a journey of expanding horizons.

Without full awareness, we have brought about a new journey. We also have chosen the destination.

If this journey had taken place in a dream, what would we have thought the destination meant? We sort through our associations—places where we have been deliriously happy, where danger lurked, where we found someone or lost someone. In a certain place, we learned something vitally important about ourselves; in a particular city or country, we experienced something that forever colors our feeling about it.

All places have meanings for us. This is true whether or not we have been there. We may have direct knowledge of those crooked streets and charming rooftops and serene sunsets. If we do, our meaning for the place will contain those elements—and many more, of course.

A place that is unknown to us still may have some associations, simply because its meaning is universal: Dark Continent, desert island, City of Light, winter wonderland. The Grand Canyon is familiar to anyone—even to people who have never seen it. Likewise Big Ben, the Eiffel Tower, and the Great Wall are familiar to people who have never been to London, Paris, or China.

The challenge for us is to sort out our connections with the place to which we have been called—seemingly by another but really, we know now, by a higher part of our selves.

Exploring the meaning of the place is the key to understanding the journey. When we have learned what the place means for us, we have discovered the way of the traveler.

A New Way of Seeing

What if this were happening in a dream? How would we interpret it?

For several years I had the opportunity of studying the approach to dream analysis developed by Carl Jung, the great Swiss psychoanalyst. Jung's dream world is a realm of myths, archetypes, storybook tales, and fables, all fueled by symbols and their universal or personal meanings.

As I learned more and more about interpreting dreams, I began to apply some of those principles to my waking life. The results were astonishing. When I found a broken window at the back of the house, instead of dismissing it as petty vandalism or the result of a wayward tree branch, I preferred to treat it as I would had it occurred in a dream: as a "breakthrough" in my "outlook." Within days, I enjoyed a tremendous leap of insight about an important aspect of my life.

I had been working exhaustingly long hours as department chair of the university where I had founded an academic program in cinema studies. Thinking about the broken window symbolically helped me realize that I could easily lighten my workload by delegating some responsibilities—and that if I did that, the department would not crack and fall apart. I knew in an instant that my role had shifted from an overworked one-man band to a calm leader who could empower others. This was a breakthrough insight for me, brought about by the broken window.

The "dream" of the broken window—opening for me a new way of seeing—symbolized the insight that would come to me. The event happened in my waking life, but I read it on another level and received a powerful message.

When you travel, whether it is to a place you have chosen for yourself or to a location that has been preordained, ask yourself: If this journey happened in a dream, how would I interpret it?

Write down your destination on a page titled "Meaning of the Place" and make a list of things you associate with that location.

If you do this for every trip you take, your path in life will come more clearly into focus.

The meaning of the place reveals the next step in my soul's journey. No trip is insignificant. Every time I am given a destination for travel, I am handed an opportunity to learn more about the meaning of my life.

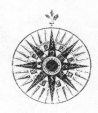

*Why do you stay here and live this mean toiling life
when a glorious existence is possible for you?
These same stars twinkle over other fields than these.*

Henry David Thoreau

Into the Unknown

Our journey lies before us like an ancient map of the known world. There is the land we recognize, and the sea, and the rest all around it is a mystery. The cartographers of old called it "terra incognita," the unknown territory.

We do not undertake the journey lightly.

Deciding to go to a place where we have never been before requires courage. After all, we are literally setting out for our personal terra incognita. With no knowledge of our destination, we are like those ancient explorers who stared at their dragon-bordered maps and wondered whether it was at all wise to tempt fate.

Even going to a place that we have visited before calls for fortitude. We have been there, so we know, generally, what to expect. But new things we might uncover on this particular trip are not known to us.

To leave home in the first place is an act of bravery. Many people opt never to do it or to do it as infrequently as possible. We understand that leaving the comforts of where we are and what we know is not easy. Transformation is never easy—and transformation is what the journey promises.

We weigh the pros and cons of leaving home. On the side of staying here is the life we are familiar with—our home, our loved ones, our animal companions, and the simple pleasures of our daily routine.

On the side of leaving home is the possibility of discovery, and with it the thrill of adventure. Journeying, we have the opportunity of finding the answers to questions we have had at home. Going out, we might unearth nuggets of happiness and harmony that have been eluding us in this place.

In spite of our fears, we decide to leave.

We do this with awareness. We know full well that the road is fraught with dangers—that emotional highwaymen may be hiding in the shadows, that dragons of confusion and anxiety may rise in our path to threaten us. As we navigate our way through the waves, the sea may end abruptly.

No one departs on a journey without some anxiety. Fear of the unknown is an essential part of our human program. If we were perfectly fearless, we could find ourselves in trouble at every turn.

Rational fear is appropriate and can even be a gift. It encourages us to be circumspect—surely one of the qualities that leads to true awareness.

We must not allow irrational fear to take over, however. Fear of that sort can overwhelm us and severely limit the progress of our journey, preventing vitally important lessons from reaching us.

The Dragon That Wasn't There

Fear is sharp-sighted, as Cervantes observed four hundred years ago. It can create mirages in our imagination, convincing us that something dangerous is lurking there, when nothing is there at all.

True, we never know before we begin a journey how we will fare along the way to our destination and along the way home. Challenges can be waiting for us behind every rock and thicket and tree in the forest. Ogres can appear out of the shadows when we least expect them. But to stay at home because we cannot be certain of a completely carefree journey seems rather lifeless and dull. If we give in to a fear of what might be "out there"— outside of our comfort zone—we deprive ourselves of the tremendous joys and powerful lessons of the journey.

Our travels most likely will not go entirely as planned. Knowing beforehand all the twists and turns of our voyage is like knowing before we open it what is inside the gift box with the fancy wrapping paper and the ribbons. Often the occasional "mishap" on the road turns instead into a rich encounter that offers an outstanding opportunity for personal growth.

Something in us does not want to live our lives on the couch. Part of being human is the desire to discover what lies over the next hill, to try to see beyond the horizon. We were born with a strong sense of daring at the center of our souls. Although we feel apprehension at the prospect of going into the unknown, the possibility of discovery almost always dispels it.

Ambrose Redmoon says, "Courage is not the absence of fear, but rather the judgment that something else is more important than fear."

Cervantes's Don Quixote goes out to fight dragons on the Spanish plains. But what he thinks are dragons are actually windmills. The dragons exist only in the mind of the romantically inclined knight.

Sometimes we see dragons that are not really there. We hear rumors about the dangers of the road, and we begin to believe them. We envision troubles, from potholes to thieves, and we imagine ourselves having to deal with them, perhaps being helpless in the face of them.

Remember, they are windmills, not dragons.

We go on our mighty expedition of self-discovery not because it is easy, and not because we are completely free from concern, but because we are compelled at the deepest level of our being to find the treasure that is waiting for us at journey's end.

Going with Confidence

Before I undertake any trip, I try to identify my fears—whether rational or irrational—and I consign them to a "Fear Box."

You can do the same. Whenever you begin to feel trip apprehension creeping up behind you, sit down with a pen and paper. At the top, on one side, write "Rational Fears," and on the other side, "Irrational Fears."

Under "Rational Fears" list things that you are concerned about. For one trip, you might write down: I don't know the language—I could be misunderstood or taken advantage of; I can't depend on the quality of tap water for drinking; I don't know where clinics or doctors' offices are in case of an unforeseen health problem.

These are all legitimate concerns, and many of them can be addressed easily before you leave. You can learn a few basic words of the foreign language, so you will not feel helpless at your destination. You can find out ahead of time about water quality and the location of medical facilities by checking guidebooks or making a few simple phone calls.

Under "Irrational Fears," you might jot down something like: I could take the wrong bus and never find the way back to the hotel; I might befriend someone who will then steal my belongings; I'll surely cause a traffic incident because of inexperience driving on the left side of the road.

These are fears for which there is no support in reality. It is absurd, for instance, to believe that taking the wrong bus will make one lost forever. No thief is lying in wait to steal, using the cover of friendship to gain one's confidence. And traffic incidents will depend entirely on your driving skills and your attention to the rules of the road.

Now here is the interesting part of the exercise. On the sheet of paper, cross out—rather emphatically—all of the irrational fears. They don't exist anymore. Then take each of the legitimate fears and write each one on a separate slip of paper. These go into your Fear Box.

At last, all your fears about the journey are contained in one place. From time to time before you leave home, open the box and check each fear to see if it is still an appropriate concern. If you handled the matter to your satisfaction, rip the "fear" up and throw it away.

By the time you begin your journey, practically all of your fears will have evaporated. Some will be left, however. Seal up the box and leave it at home. When you are out in the world on your journey of self-discovery, you will be aware that the fears you once had are not along with you. They are closed up in a box, incapable of being part of your experience on the road.

The road stretches out before me. I know I will encounter obstacles. The path will sometimes appear circuitous, or worse, perilous. I have fears. But still, I go.

May the road rise with you and the wind be ever at your back.

Irish Toast

The Decision to Go

The gods of travel beckoned us—and we responded.

Now we resolve to undertake the journey.

In the decision to quit this place and go out into the world is the promise of change. Here, in this definitive act of the will, is the seed of our transformation. In spite of our apprehensions, real or imagined, in the face of the unknown, and regardless of the inconveniences, difficulties, and unpredictable demands of the road, we choose to leave all of the comforts of home behind. We decide to go.

The young Siddhattha Gotama received the intuitive call to find out what might be "out there" beyond the walls of his splendid palace. He decided to leave the comforts of his father's house. In Buddhist tradition this sacred determination is called the great "Going Forth." Once Siddhattha made his decision, he set in motion a whole vast theater of change that would end with his own enlightenment.

In our own quest, we feel a heady rush of excitement from making this courageous decision to act. Nothing will ever be the same, for we have begun the unalterable course to self-discovery.

At the beginning, when we first heard the call to journey in a dream, we wondered at it. Perhaps we were caught off guard and tried to dismiss it. But the call was too strong—the pull too powerful. The decision to go was still far off, but a restlessness of the spirit had dawned in us.

Fear stopped us in our steps momentarily. We imagined confusions and fierce dragons—emotional, psychological, and spiritual—that might block our way. As we looked closely at each of those fears, however, and saw that they were mostly groundless, they began to shrivel up and disappear. They flew away on the winds of enthusiasm that were sweeping over us.

Now there is only the bright promise of the journey and the doing of it. I have decided to make this journey, we have said to ourselves—and then we have repeated it aloud. We have told our families and our loved ones. In announcing our intention, we have activated the process of going and finding, and of bringing back, the great gift of self-knowledge.

A Travel Shrine

One of the most important ways to work spiritually with a journey is to create a travel shrine.

Your shrine to your journey is an incarnation—a presentation in the outer world of what has been going on inside you since you first dreamed of making a trip. It is a tangible expression of the journey in all its many manifestations, including your excitement, your hesitations, your preparations, and your expectations.

You will find many wonderful uses for the travel shrine, but its primary function is to help you to visualize all the issues that surround your journey. Now, when you have reached the point of decision—when you know that you will be making the journey—this is the time to create your shrine.

Shrines have been with us for eons. They stretch far back into antiquity, perhaps to the very dawn of human consciousness. Wherever traces of early civilizations have been uncovered, shrines and altars, prayer panels, and sanctuaries have been found. They are a way of externalizing the sense of reverence and wonder we have inside.

I begin creating my travel shrine at the moment I resolve to answer the call to journey. I clear a large shelf in my office, lay down a plain white cloth, and install my first honored article—a simple candle. For me, the candle is a symbol of the entire journey, from the period of preparation straight through to my homecoming. More, it represents my willingness to engage the journey. The candle says that I am answering the call of my higher consciousness to fearlessly seek new self-knowledge.

As the days and weeks progress toward my date of departure, I bring more articles of significance to my shrine. If I am going to a place I have never visited, I find pictures of that place and stand them up on my shrine. If I am going to a foreign country, I try to get a few bills or coins of that country's currency and place them on the shrine.

On one journey a few years ago, I was returning to the little town where I grew up. I had been gone from there for almost thirty years and did not know what to expect. Would I even recognize the people and places I knew so well when I was a child growing up there?

My travel shrine for that journey was laden with class pictures from grade school—group photographs featuring a sea of innocent faces surrounding a half-remembered teacher. I placed other mementos on my

Symbols of the Journey

Make a list of what you will place on your travel shrine. Are there people in your life you want to entrust to the gods of the journey? What are the things that you consider sacred in your life right now, deserving of a place on your altar? What else of meaning will you raise to a spiritual level through inclusion in your shrine?

This is also an opportunity to look upon your journey as an inner expedition in search of self-knowledge. Include in your list a few personal items that symbolize a change you would like to make in your life, or matter you are seeking clarity about. A little heart might stand for a relationship, of which you seek a deeper understanding. A piece of jewelry might represent the riches of the world that you deserve but have been preventing yourself from obtaining. These are symbols of the journey within—tokens that remind you that all your travels are movement toward higher self-awareness. These items have a special place on your travel shrine.

shrine's altar: a playbill with my name on it; a small sack of marbles; an essay written in pencil, which sported a small gold star; a printed invitation to my eighth-grade graduation; a get-well card from a beloved aunt, sent to comfort me when I had the mumps.

By the time I began my journey, which turned out to be remarkably moving and insightful, the candle I had placed there when I started my shrine was surrounded by dozens of other articles of profound meaning.

I left some room on the shrine for what I would bring to it after the trip. When I returned home with new photos of former classmates and teachers, printed invitations to reunion parties, and other fresh mementos, they went onto my travel shrine. Together, all of the articles represented the many facets of that journey.

It had been a journey of reunion for me, reuniting all the parts of my past with my present, showing me who I am by revealing what I was. All of it was there on the altar for me to see, to understand, and to love.

I make the conscious decision to leave my home and go to another place. I do this willingly and in full expectation that the rewards of self-knowledge will be mine at the end of my travels. When I decide to accept the invitation of my angel of the journey to rise to the next level of myself, all the world rushes to my side to be my companion to higher consciousness.

Part Two

The Preparation

*Though we travel the world over to find
the beautiful, we must carry it with us
or we find it not.*

Ralph Waldo Emerson

Avoiding danger is no safer in the long run than outright exposure. Life is either a daring adventure or nothing.

Helen Keller

Once the decision is made to venture forth, spiritual and material provisions appear as if by magic. It is the gods' way of rewarding the hero for the courage of assenting to undertake the journey, with all its rigors, known and unknown, as well as its rewards.

Perseus attends a banquet given by King Polydectes, the man who wants to marry his mother. Being young and a stranger to the kingdom, he arrives at the feast without a gift. As the party progresses, he frames his speech to the crowd. When his time arrives, he stands and declares that in return for the friendship of Polydectes, he will go out and find the dreaded Medusa, slay her, and bring back her head.

The boast is so bold and, some would say, so foolish that the revelers are rendered speechless and the banquet comes to a halt. Medusa is a monster with snakes for hair; anyone who looks at her face is turned immediately to stone. Others have attempted to bring her down, but they have failed—their bones litter the path to her dwelling.

But Perseus is different. He is a hero.

Next morning the young man sails out. Then, the myth tells us, the god Hermes rushes to his side with an array of special provisions he will need to find and slay Medusa, including Hermes's own winged sandals. As Perseus makes his way, often in the company of Hermes, he encounters kindhearted people, who give him more assistance. On the eve of his encounter with the monster, the great goddess Athena herself gives him nothing less than her brilliant shield. With it, he will be able to attack Medusa by staring into the monster's mirrored image on the shield and thus avoid looking her in the face.

We never go out unprotected or unprepared. There seems to be a spiritual law in this: If we answer the call to journey, which is the invitation to transform ourselves by expanding our awareness, we will be helped along the way. For those who opt to stay at home, no help comes; they are left behind with the questionable comforts they have managed to create around them, holding the world at bay. But those who agree to go forth receive everything they need, and more, to perform the task at hand.

In the myths, divine assistance comes to those who have a clear vision of what they are undertaking. Perseus has a simple goal: to bring back the head of Medusa. Jason has an equally simple objective: to return home with the Golden Fleece. Theseus has a burning desire to rid the kingdom of the menace of the Minotaur.

In the Cinderella story, the young girl wants to go to the ball, a metaphor for going out into the world. At the ball she will find her prince, the male half of herself—she will bring about the integration of her personality. To accomplish this feat, she needs to be transformed. Her intention to engage the quest is so powerful that she draws to herself supernatural assistance—a fairy godmother—who provides everything she requires to go to the ball.

When we venture into the world with the intention to discover as much as we can about ourselves, the gods prepare the way for us. We have only to be sincere in our quest and give ourselves without reservation to the process of our transformation. Everything in the world heeds our noble intention.

The heroes obtain supernatural support not only for the great encounter with the monster, but also for the journey that leads to that encounter and leads back home. Theseus, responding to a humanitarian impulse to end the slaughter of youths and maidens by the Minotaur, is given the means to find his way out of the Labyrinth. Lovely Ariadne gives him a ball of string to unwind as he goes into the insoluble maze to meet the monster. Tracing the string back after he performs his heroic task, he is able to reach the entrance again.

On our epic journey of self-discovery, we need the mental, emotional, and spiritual wherewithal to leave home, to bravely face the ogres that have been impeding our progress, and then to find our way back to where we started. We also need to prepare for the journey with material provisions we will use or give to others we meet on our path.

The gods will help. On a deeper level, the myths tell us that these otherworldly provisions are well within our reach. In fact, they are closer to us than we had imagined: they are within us.

The spiritual path . . . is simply the journey of living our lives.
Marianne Williamson

Spiritual Provisions

On the road, we are likely to encounter many adventures. To sustain us on the way, to fortify us for our fateful meetings with new people in new places, we will need provisions.

Now it is time to reflect and choose the goods we will want at hand along the road, and to assemble them.

Before the great heroes of mythology left home on their epic quests, they gathered everything they needed to assure the achievement of their goals. Whether it was to slay a dragon, behead a monster, outsmart an angry goddess, or find the Holy Grail, they wanted to be prepared for the journey. Into their enchanted bags went special potions, three-headed guard dogs, magic ropes, golden arrows, talking seashells, and the rest.

These were the indispensable tools of the trip, without which a hero would not dare to go far from home.

The myths speak in the language of poetry. If a hero sets out with a shield that renders her invincible, we might say that she is protected by superhuman courage. If a hero carries a mirror that induces hypnotism in all who gaze upon it, that might be a metaphor for a mesmerizing charm.

These are more than mere physical necessities for the trip. They are spiritual provisions. As we prepare for our travels, we ask: Does it not make sense to bring along spiritual provisions to meet spiritual challenges and fill spiritual needs? This journey is ultimately an inner journey. We assemble spiritual provisions for this wondrous trek deep into the heart of ourselves—or to assist us in conducting our adventure in the world.

Only the appropriate provisions will do. For this journey we must be swift of foot. We stop now and ponder what spiritual stores serve us and what might be simply unwanted baggage.

Fear not. In this momentous enterprise, we are prompted and guided by our gods of travel.

Virtues and Values

I have found it helpful to approach the idea of spiritual provisions for a trip in the most mundane and "nonspiritual" way imaginable. I try to anticipate what I will need in terms of virtues and values, and I simply pack them in with my physical belongings.

You can spiritualize your own travel in the same way.

This is how I happened upon the idea of spiritual provisions. A few years ago, when I found myself traveling several days out of every month, I started the practice of packing with the help of a list. Instead of stuffing my suitcases blindly and hoping for the best, I wrote a list beforehand of all the items of clothing and other things I would need while I was away from home.

After making several successful trips using this method, I began thinking about what else I might need for my journeys. I was not thinking of clothes or shaving equipment or shoe polish, but of something intangible—something I might not be able to see and touch, but that I could sense in another way, and that would be every bit as necessary for my travels as shoes and razors.

That is when I had the idea of packing in with my clothes a simple card that said "Courage."

Some time ago, when I visited family members after a long absence, I packed notes that said "Fortitude" and "Good humor" and "Compassion."

Travel Provisions

How have you prepared yourself for life's journey up to this point? Are you carrying with you some unnecessary baggage, such as other people's ideas of who you are?

Explore what you need and what you do not need to make your life journey a perfect experience. List what you would not like to take along, such as old hurts and resentments, poor decisions, and broken promises.

Now list what you would like to take with you—positive, intangible belongings such as memories of your triumphs and feelings of accomplishment.

Add to this list the virtues and values you will pack with you for your journey.

As it turned out, I needed every single one of those spiritual attributes during the journey—and they were there for me.

You are the hero of your own journey. Every time you leave home on a trip, you are embarking on a quest for self-knowledge. The spiritual provisions you bring with you are, like that extra sweater in case the weather turns or the swimsuit in case the hotel has a pool, a kind of insurance for the success of the trip on the spiritual level.

Try this: If you are making a business trip, pack "Bravery" and "Justice" in with your socks, shoes, and toiletries. If you are going off to visit a friend you have not seen for a long time, pack "Kindness" and "Beauty" and "Truth" into the zippered pockets of your suitcase. On a trip to begin a new chapter in your life, take along "Daring."

Here is a short list of some spiritual qualities that might make good provisions for your next journey. Write each word on a separate sheet of high-quality paper, fold, and seal—maybe with sealing wax and your own crest, just to make it official-looking and even more sacred.

Forgiveness	Cheerfulness
Charm	Self-Esteem
Willingness to Listen	Mental Clarity
Tact	Openness to Change
Strength	Generosity of Spirit
Honesty	Flexibility

Before she left on a recent journey, an artist friend of mine finally got up the courage to pack the one important spiritual provision she had been leaving at home. Quite unexpectedly, during a trip that was supposed to have been a simple private showing for a new client, she met her future husband.

The night before her journey, she had packed away "Love."

In preparing for my journey of self-discovery, I pack
spiritual provisions that I will need along the way.
The virtues and values I bring give me courage and strength—
and are a spiritual blessing to those I encounter on my adventure.

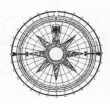

There is an expression—walking with beauty. And I believe that this endless search for beauty in surroundings, in people, and in one's personal life, is the headstone of travel.

Juliette de Bairacli Levy, *Traveler's Joy*

Goals of the Journey

The goal of our journey is not necessarily the same as the reason we have for making it.

Often, the reason for traveling is given to us beforehand. It is present in the seed of the journey to which we are called: to witness a wedding, to comfort a friend, to conclude an agreement, to attend a reunion. At other times, the reason is more vague—we may simply need a respite from daily routine or crave a change of scene.

But the reason for our journey may not be the same as the goal of our wanderings. Even when we know the reason for travel, we still can choose our personal goal. And so, we ask, what do we want to accomplish for ourselves on this journey?

When we heard the first faint call to leave home and go off on an adventure, we caught the echo of a goal and a purpose. Since that time, we have searched our heart repeatedly. We want to learn why we have been pulled away from home and toward this experience.

Now we are beginning to understand that the primary goal of our journey is to bring something back.

We go out to find and recover that which has been lost, or that has been missing in our lives.

First and last, the goal of our wanderings is to bring back a higher and richer knowledge of ourselves.

The heroes of old went out to conquer monsters, which we understand represent the ferocious beasts of their own lower natures. They sailed forth to perform Olympian labors, which is akin to the interior work we do to improve ourselves. They struck out on their bold adventures to bring back the prize, which we know is profound self-knowledge, leading to wisdom.

We are the heroes of our own journey. On our travels, we strive to accomplish our own inner Herculean tasks.

And our goal is that which we understand will bring us closer to what makes us whole. We may aspire to compassion, to generosity, to forgiveness, to love. We may strive for balance, for kindness, for release from false appetites, for acceptance. These make the quest worthwhile and elevate it to the realm of the sacred.

The goals of our journey are ours. We choose them, and we act upon them. And when, on this journey of the heart, we attain them, we complete ourselves.

Bring Awareness

You can accomplish goals on your journey that will enhance your life immeasurably upon your return.

All you need is three small blank cards and a willingness to bring awareness into your travel.

A friend of mine who travels a great deal tells me that he never leaves home without asking himself what he considers the most obvious door-closing question in the world: Why am I doing this?

The first answer he receives is what he considers "the reason for the trip." But he doesn't stop there. He considers the reason for a trip to be quite inconsequential—a simple pretext for getting him away from home and on the road. The more important answer to his question has to do with goals. He rephrases the question to, "What do I want this trip to mean for me?"

You can make a journey mean anything at all. If you travel consciously, you will want to make it mean something that will help you learn more about yourself.

Your goals can be general, such as attaining self-knowledge or conquering fear or learning compassion. They can also be quite specific. You may want to accomplish patience or self-acceptance or a higher appreciation of beauty.

All these goals are attainable.

Remember that you have within you the power to accomplish any goal you set out to attain. To do this, it is necessary to set your goals before the journey as part of your preparation.

As you prepare for a trip, formulate three goals. Keep them simple. They may be as simple as these: stop worrying about my appearance, listen to people more carefully, and choose food I have never tasted before.

Write these goals out on three-by-five-inch cards and place them on your travel shrine. Then, the night before you leave, tape them side-by-side to the inside of your suitcase. While on the trip, you won't be able to avoid them. You'll look at them every time you need a change of clothes, a new file folder, or your favorite book.

With your goals always before you, you are constantly reminded of your journey's true purpose—to accomplish the key aims you have chosen for yourself.

My journey is mine. The goals I would accomplish on my journey are mine. I will bring back the Golden Fleece of my own perfected self. The goals I choose direct me to the center of my being. In that secret, sacred place, I dwell serenely, full of the understanding that comes with wisdom.

*Go lightly, simply. Too much seriousness clouds the soul.
Just go, and follow the flowing moment. Try not to cling to
any experience. The depths of wonder open of themselves.*

Frederick Lehrman

Material Provisions

To make our journey, we also need material goods.

An empty purse will not get us far along the road. Without money, we cannot progress from one place to another. Without money, we may not be able to return home. Indeed, we may not even be able to leave home.

At least, this is what conventional wisdom tells us.

But we are conscious travelers. We look for a more profound meaning in the notion of material provisions.

Serious advice found in a distinguished nineteenth-century travel book: "Never take a trip you can afford."

How do we reconcile that seemingly paradoxical but seemingly sound counsel against what we know to be the exigencies of travel? For are we not aware that we will need to spend money to buy fares of passage, to sustain ourselves while we are away, and to provide for our return journey? Even the heroes of mythology needed coins to pay Charon, the ferryman of the Underworld, to take them over the River Styx into the Elysian Fields.

The Buddha himself counseled his lay followers to be mindful with their finances, to invest wisely, to put money aside for the good care of their dependents, and to give alms to pilgrims on the road. Jesus, when asked about how money fit into a spiritual journey, taught his followers to, "Render unto Caesar the things that are Caesar's"—to live in the real world of money and other material provisions while pursuing the life of the spirit.

And yet, something compels us to look ever deeper at this puzzle.

At the root of the issue of material provisions is our fear that we will not have enough. Not only enough money, but enough other material supplies—clothes, utensils, books and magazines, even food.

Fear can paralyze us. It can prevent us from taking the next step on the journey. If we remain locked in the fear that we do not have enough, that we will run out, we surely will limit the parameters of our adventure.

When we decide to travel consciously, we spiritualize our journey. All that we assemble of material provisions for the trip must fall under the law of spirit—which is infinite and abundant beyond measure.

We remember the call of the journey.

In the first stirring to travel, the seed was present. And in the seed was all that would be required for the entire arc of the journey—the leaving, the exploring, the returning. Everything necessary to the journey would be provided.

The history of the world's religions shows the students of the great masters being sent out to teach people in other lands about the spiritual principles they have learned. Invariably, they are sent out penniless, with "neither rod, nor staff, nor purse." They are on a spiritual mission. On such a mission, spirit will furnish every necessity as it arises.

One of the most stirring scenes in the Bible is the great Exodus, or the "Going Forth" of the Israelites from Egypt—a spiritual journey of colossal proportions. Seen in metaphorical terms, it is the epic passage of the soul from the bondage of human limitation to the higher awareness of spiritual freedom.

When the Israelites flee their slavery, they do so quickly and take very little with them. Soon, the small amount of food they brought along is gone, but they continue bravely on their way. After wandering in the desert for weeks, they are exhausted and on the point of starvation. Now a mysterious substance begins to fall from the heavens; they eat it and are satisfied. This manna from heaven appears miraculously every day to feed an entire nation traveling to the Promised Land. And this is the spiritual lesson: the people are told to eat their fill, but not to put away any of the manna for the next day. Every day they must trust that the Divine source that beckoned them on this journey will provide for them.

Centuries later the teacher Jesus, speaking to a crowd of hundreds of hungry people in the hills of ancient Palestine, hands out twelve loaves of bread that seem to multiply miraculously. He holds in his awareness the metaphysical truth that in an abundant universe no one has to go without. His belief that travelers on a spiritual journey will always be provided for feeds the multitudes.

On our own journey, we can rest in that same sense of trust. We have assembled our material provisions to the best of our ability. If we need something more, we trust that it will appear. When we prepare for this journey, we are responding to a call from our higher nature to venture forth and find new knowledge about ourselves. It is a noble quest. We, too, must assume that, under these circumstances, the universe will conspire to assist us.

We attend to our material provisions, of course. We are human. It would be foolish for us to ignore our bodily needs. But we do not dwell on them. We have faith that everything will be supplied—if not as we leave home, then at many points along the path to our destination, and on the same path back.

For we are pilgrims on the road to higher consciousness.

We have answered a sacred call from deep within.

Where we walk, abundance goes before us.

An Abundant Universe

Acknowledging the necessity of material provisions—especially money—is the great reality check of travel.

The challenge in preparing financially at this time is to not allow money, or the lack of it, to limit your journey. You can meet this challenge in a simple and creative way.

I have learned over the years that it is foolhardy to allow extremes to rule here. To deny that you need money and other material provisions for a trip is just as absurd as being overly concerned—sometimes to the point of immobility—about having every single penny in hand before leaving home.

Rather than taking either of those two routes, I have found it useful to confront the issue head-on. You can do this, too.

Take a few dollar bills, or a few bills in the currency of the country to which you are traveling, and a handful of coins, and place them on your travel shrine. For me, this simple act of giving money to the gods of my journey makes a powerful statement. It says, "I am fully aware that I need money to make this trip—and here it is."

If I find that I do not have the money I estimate it will take to make this particular trip, I give money to the shrine anyway. Somehow that seems to prime the pump, and later financial needs work themselves out.

The spiritual principle at work here is this: in an abundant universe, there is always enough. Try to stay in that place mentally, emotionally, and spiritually before, during, and after your trip.

When you work with the issues of your journey on a spiritual level, look for miracles to happen.

*The loving universe, which fosters my self-growth
in so many ways, also provides the wherewithal for me to
make this journey. As I realize that the journey I am on
is a spiritual one, all that I need appears before me.*

If "heaven is the Lord's," the earth is the inheritance of man, and consequently any honest traveler has the right to walk as he chooses, all over that globe which is his.

Alexandra David-Neel, *My Journey to Lhasa*

Gifts

In Biblical times, the Three Wise Men packed their saddlebags with gold, frankincense, and myrrh before setting out on their long, arduous journey to Bethlehem.

They were wise, indeed. Gifting is one of the highest purposes of our travel. Giving a gift is the act of offering part of ourselves to another. A gift stays at the new place and allows a piece of us, therefore, to stay there in a mystical way.

When we give something to another person, we are making many statements. We are saying, in the first place, that we regard the person as worthy to be receiving something from us. And the gift works in two ways: as a token of esteem for the other and as a symbol of self-esteem for us.

Among the ancients, gift-giving was so important that it was ritualized and codified. When an ambassador from the king left his country to visit the ruler of a neighboring kingdom, dazzling gifts were assembled beforehand, then provisions were made for their transportation, and finally for their presentation at court. At every step of the way, prescribed ceremonials were strictly observed.

Temple walls of old Egypt are inscribed with the records of royal visits, during which huge storehouses had to be erected to stockpile the vast number of gifts that had been bestowed upon the crown. Arches and columns in Rome tell stories of imperial visitations that lasted for many weeks—time spans that were necessary to allow for ritual gift giving on a colossal scale.

We have stories also about travelers who gave gifts less grand but just as meaningful. Orpheus wandered the world of myth singing and playing his lyre, and all who heard him swooned with pleasure and delight. Even rocks came alive when he passed by strumming and singing. Pluto, God of the Underworld, burst into tears when he heard the divine music of Orpheus— it was enough for the god to allow the hero's bride, Eurydice, to return to the land of the living.

Other stories tell of travelers who gave not expensive things but gifts of the heart. The Little Drummer Boy plays a song; the Juggler throws balls into the air and catches them as entertainment for a statue of the Virgin; Johnny Appleseed goes from farm to farm reciting stories and giving out seeds that will grow into fine fruit trees.

As we prepare for the journey, we do not forget the gift.

Giving something that is ours will be essential as we progress along the road, when we reach our destination, and on our way back home. We will assemble our gifts now; we will not go forth empty-handed.

When we give, a marvelous and mysterious dance is set in motion. Giving makes it possible for the other to return a gift. Although we do not impart gifts for this reason, the pattern of give and take is established— the dance has begun.

The dance of gift-giving is karmic in nature. It is rooted in the principle of cause and effect. When we give to another, we are giving, in a roundabout way, back to ourselves. This is what Walt Whitman alludes to when he says, "The gift is to the giver, and comes back most to him—it cannot fail."

Like the kings and queens of long ago, we prepare our gifts before the journey. We will give something meaningful, something that will endure.

We give out of our abundance, in gratitude for new friendship, new vistas, and new knowledge. We give because we are thankful for new insights about ourselves—hard-won, graciously conferred.

Acts of Generosity

Gathering a few small gifts is an important part of preparing for your trip. Gifts for people we may meet on the journey need not be expensive—in fact, expensive gifts probably should be avoided—but they should be as personal as possible and evocative of the place you represent.

Many years ago, traveling in Mexico, I admired a blue scarf that my guide, an archaeology student, was wearing. A moment later, the student had presented the scarf to me as a gift.

Giving

What gifts have you given? What gifts have you received? List some gifts you have received recently, from whom, and how they showed the giver's regard for you. Now do the same with gifts you have given to others.

Imagine that the five or six most important people in your life were coming to a party you were giving. At the party, you present each of the people with an intangible gift—a sunset, courage, soft spring rain, peace of mind, and so on. What would those gifts be, and who would receive them?

This act of generosity astonished me and left me somewhat at a loss for words. Then my traveling companion explained that manners in this culture dictated that some small thing admired by a new friend be given to him as a way to seal the friendship.

For a long time afterward, I wore the blue scarf. Every time I did, I was reminded of the person who gave it to me—eventually I forgot the guide's name—and that sunny day exploring the ruins of an ancient Mayan settlement.

The scarf has ended up in a trunk that I keep for just such items. I call it my travel treasure chest. When I want to revisit a place in my imagination, I open the treasure chest and sift through its contents. A hundred other gifts have joined the scarf now—each of them a tangible, vivid reminder of a particular journey.

But the scarf holds a special place in there because of the lesson it taught me. When I was handed the scarf, I took it gratefully, but I had nothing to give in return. Since then, I never leave home without something to give if the opportunity arises.

Here is a short list of things you might take along with you for gifts: snapshots of yourself, members of your family, your animal companions; postcards from your town or your state; small souvenirs from home, such as key chains or T-shirts; a copy of a favorite book; commemorative or currency coins; a hometown newspaper (this will seem quite exotic to someone in another land); a small address book—with your name and address written in as the first entry.

While packing your gifts, remember to make room in your bags to receive gifts from others.

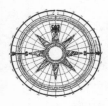

To give is why I am on this road. In giving, I receive.
It is an endless circle of bestowing and accepting. On my journey,
I am grateful for everyone who contributes to my further discovery
of myself. To honor them, to show my gratitude, I give to others
generously, out of the unending abundance of spirit within me.

Traveling is not just seeing the new; it is also leaving behind.
Not just opening doors; also closing them behind you,
never to return. But the place you have left forever is
always there for you to see whenever you shut your eyes.

Jan Myrdal, *The Silk Road*

Closing the Door

Our preparation is ended. We leave home. We close the door.

This final act symbolizes so much—and we do it with full awareness of its importance to the mystic nature of the journey.

The door closes. Behind us now is the life we know so well, with all its comforts and reassuring connections. We leave it—the cozy warm bed, the familiar faces in the pictures on the nightstand, the subtle sounds of the day, the satisfying and consoling scents of this place.

We leave it all.

Around us, like an embrace, home is here in the present, and yet, mysteriously, it is now part of our past. Though we have not yet left home, home seems to have left us. In a peculiar way, we have outgrown it.

We may feel the sadness of leaving descend on us as we stare at the door. Looking at it from this side, the inside, we are still here. When we look at it from the other side—from the outside—we will have gone. This place, home, will be empty. It will exist for us then only in memory.

Closure is essential to the journey. Nothing can happen without it.

In 1519, Hernán Cortés and his party of Spanish adventurers sailed over the Atlantic and arrived on the coast of Mexico. They set anchor in the New World at a town they named Vera Cruz, "the True Cross." For a week they explored the region and heard stories of fabulous empires to the west. Then Cortés sent out a remarkable, harrowing order: Burn the ships.

For the soldiers under his command, those proud galleons were like home. More than that, really—for the ships were the only means to take them back to their true homes. Setting torches to them must have taken immense courage, coupled with an unwavering faith in their commander.

But Cortés had prepared them for the order. He had painted a picture of the new, undiscovered lands that lay beyond the mountains and the jungles, awash in riches. To stay behind would be comfortable, of course, but cowardly. To forge ahead would lead them on the road to excitement, fame, and the promise of unimaginable fortunes in gold.

Once they had destroyed their ships—closing the door forever upon a precipitous departure, initiating their journey of discovery—they opened the possibility of glory. In a month's time they would encounter the resplendent Aztec prince, Montezuma. And the history of western civilization would be changed forever.

We are like those bold explorers. In all of metaphysical literature, gold is the symbol for spiritual riches. To find that gold, we abandon everything we know and march forth from home. We burn our ships.

We close the door.

All travel is inner travel. The end of preparation is the beginning of the journey. We are a step away from the first halting movement toward the thrilling adventure that will end in self-discovery.

We have accepted the call. We take the step that leads away from home. We close the door.

Over the Threshold

When you leave on a trip, the last act you perform on the way out of the house—both in a literal and figurative sense—is closing the door.

After many years of travel, I discovered a wonderfully effective spiritual exercise to assure that my trip will be a conscious one. You may want to try it for yourself. It is so simple that it hardly seems like an exercise at all.

I make leaving my house a ceremonial event.

First, I spend some time on the day before I leave thinking about two or three small things I associate with home—things I see and use every day in the house. I usually come up with articles such as a favorite coffee mug, a set of keys, a leather bookmark, a pen I keep by the phone for messages.

On the morning of travel day, I take these items and place them on my travel shrine. Symbolically, I am presenting my "comforts of home" to my gods of travel. Here they (and therefore a part of me) will be kept safe all during my journey.

I see this also as an act of blessing. By offering the tokens of home to my shrine, I feel that I am thanking and blessing everything I am leaving behind at home.

Finally, I approach the door. I open it and take my suitcases outside. Now part of me is already on the journey. I am in two worlds.

I come back into the house, position myself at the door, and walk over the threshold, this time with an intense awareness that I am making a crossing. At last, I close the door behind me. I turn and look at the closed door.

Now, truly, I have left home. My journey has begun.

So long ago, I heard the call of the journey. It beckoned to me in a dream. With all the courage I could muster, I answered the call. Now I close the door forever on the past of myself. I walk into the future. Here, new knowing waits for me; new doors open to me.

Part Three

The Encounter

The months and days are the travelers of eternity.
The years that come and go are also voyagers.
I too for years past have been stirred by the sight of a solitary
cloud drifting with the wind to ceaseless thoughts of roaming.

Matsuo Basho, *The Narrow Road to Oku*

I do believe that the outward and the inward life correspond. . . .
To set about living a true life is to go on a journey to a distant
country, gradually to find ourselves surrounded by new scenes
and men; and as long as the old are around me, I know that
I am not in any true sense living a new or a better life.

Henry David Thoreau, Letter to Harrison Blake, 1848

The encounter is the centerpiece of the journey.

Arriving at the destination, the hero takes the lay of the land, regards the situation, and determines what is to be done. Now the hour has come. Now is the realization of the dream, the fulfillment of the promise. The call to journey was about this time, the meticulous preparation was about this time. Something momentous will happen here, and after that, nothing will be the same—everything will be different.

For the heroes of myth, the encounter is the moment of truth. Perseus catches sight of the horrible Medusa reflected in his shield. He takes aim with his sword, reaches behind him, avoids gazing upon her face, and slices through her neck. It is done.

In the dark shadows of the Labyrinth, a terrifying silence. Then behind him, Theseus hears the snort of the ghastly Minotaur, half-man, half-bull. He turns with sword bared, and with one mighty thrust through the heart, brings the monster down. The heroic deed is accomplished.

The ancients, who created the grand myths and handed them down to the generations that followed, understood the hero's adventures as symbolic of our individual feats of daring as we confront and deal with the many facets of life. If the epic journey of the spirit leads to a place deep inside ourselves, then we can look upon the exploits of the mythical heroes as expeditions to meet and destroy the "monster" within. What are those monsters? How did they get there, and why are they still plaguing the countryside of our personalities?

One way of thinking about the inner monster is as an obstruction, real or imagined, that has been keeping us from expressing our true selves. The obstruction can be physical, mental, or emotional. It can be something as simple as a chronic backache, or as complex as paranoia. It can be merely irritating, such as thinking of one's self as failure-prone, or utterly incapacitating, such as assuming the role of a victim in all areas of one's life. Once the obstacle is brought into the light of consciousness—like Theseus finding the Minotaur in the darkness of the Labyrinth—it is easier to overcome. In fact, seeing the monster clearly, as Perseus beheld the Medusa in the brilliant light of Athena's shield, and facing it unafraid is most of the work of subduing it.

When we travel in the world "out there," we are also making a hero's journey to the heart of our being. Passing through the obstacle on the path is the purpose of the epic journey. Sometimes we come across real, tangible obstacles on our journey, and have to work through them—sometimes the obstructions are emotional or psychological. Making our way through them to the other side makes us stronger—it makes us whole.

When that is done, the hero can begin the trek home. Then, in so many of the myths, on the way back from meeting the monster, the hero comes across a "stranger." And the stranger has a riddle for the hero to solve. This encounter is a kind of mental puzzle, the thinking counterpart to the physical challenge of confronting the monster.

The stranger seems to be a metaphor for the hero, but in a transformed state—the hero who has answered the call to higher self-awareness, who has prepared for an encounter with obstacles to personal growth, and who has moved through those obstructions. The stranger is "strange" because the hero has not yet fully realized that the great change has occurred. In solving the riddle proposed by the stranger (the hero always solves it), the way is made clear for the triumphal homecoming.

Travel transforms us—it is almost a cliché to say it, but it is one of the towering truths of life. When we close the door of home upon the past, we open another door to personal transformation. At the heart of that journey "out," we happen upon the deepest mysteries "within." There, the possibility of realizing the highest version of self lies waiting—waiting for us to recognize it, claim it, and begin on the path back home victorious.

Afoot and light-hearted I take to the open road,
Healthy, free, the world before me,
The long brown path before me leading wherever I choose.
Henceforth I ask not good-fortune, I myself am good-fortune.

Walt Whitman, "Song of the Open Road"

Getting There

Suddenly, we are on the journey.

It has not truly come suddenly, but only seems so. We have prepared for weeks, perhaps months. We have waited for this moment since we heard the faint call to journey in a dream, and that may have been long ago.

Too often we think the journey will begin when we arrive at our destination. But getting to that destination is also part of the journey. In fact, it may be the most important part. When we turn to our rich cultural heritage of myth, literature, and history, we find that always and everywhere the approach to the destination has been regarded as sacred.

Medieval cathedrals were designed with the concept of the approach foremost in the minds and hearts of the builders. We look at a magnificent cathedral from above, seeing it as a bird sees it: as a cross, with the entrance at the foot and the place of the unfolding mysteries deep inside, at the crossing. From the cathedral's entrance to the crossing is the long walk to the heart of faith—the approach.

Ancient civilizations made the processional an indispensable part of every holy ceremony. In the ruins of the forums and markets of the ancient world we discover the remains of wide avenues constructed for the all-important ceremonial approach. Trajan's Column, one of the greatest remnants of Rome's glorious imperial past, is the carved record of one long procession that celebrated the "divine" emperor's life and his contributions to the state.

Mayan, Aztec, and Toltec ceremonial cities in the Americas were planned around processional pathways, along which entire populations would move to the place of sacred rites. Egyptian royal mourners marched in solemn procession up long ramps in the Valley of the Kings. Greeks paraded through festooned marketplaces waving banners and palm fronds on their way to temples to honor their gods.

Throughout history, the act of moving in the direction of the destination has been profoundly significant.

So it is for us. We make ourselves aware at every moment that we are moving steadily toward the aim of our journey.

"The journey is its own destination," states an old proverb. All travel on the way to our goal is a consecrated activity.

We know that the process of the journey is itself the journey. Every step we take tells us something more about who we are.

We proceed to our destination.

And as we walk, the procession transforms us.

Magical Steps

Like most of us, I used to travel with only my destination in mind. The last thing that occurred to me was to try to appreciate how I was approaching that destination and to learn what meaning that approach was giving to my travels.

Now, as a conscious traveler, I want to be aware of all the phases of my journey, from the moment I leave my house until the moment I return to it. All the steps between those two points are present with me as I go to where I am going and as I come back.

Here is what I call the "Really" activity. It has helped me to be present in the going and in the coming back. Try it once or twice a day while approaching your destination. You will find that your adventure is vastly enhanced.

Take a moment and close your eyes. Ask yourself two questions: Where am I right now, really? Where am I going, really?

You may be on a plane flying over the Mississippi River. If so, answer yourself with that information. You may be going to a wedding. That is your answer to the second question.

That would be enough to anchor you to the process of the journey. But there is more to this deceptively elementary exercise.

As you rest with these questions and answers, something deeper seems to set in. The word "really" begins to work. You may have the thought that you are on your way to encounter yourself. The wedding, although it is an external event, may symbolize for you the marriage between disparate parts of yourself, out of which you become an integrated personality. The crossing of the river may rise in your thoughts as an archetypal crossing, like passing over the Rubicon, or the Delaware, or the Red Sea; crossing a river comes to symbolize crossing into a new area of your personality—you can never go back.

This exercise works for all kinds of travel to any destination. You can make your journey a hero's quest if you just ask yourself where you really are right now and where it is that you are really going.

The "Really" activity has never failed to open my eyes to my true destination and to the magical steps that are taking me to it.

I have left my home. I have not yet arrived at the goal of my yearnings. Now I am in the place between places. My journey, I see, is not only my destination. It resides at every station along the way. And at each stop I have the opportunity to be created anew.

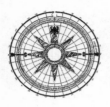

Wherever your journey takes you, there are new gods waiting there, with divine patience—and laughter.

Susan M. Watkins

Being Present

At last, we are here.

We have dreamed of this place, and we have prepared ourselves well for coming. Now, with a full, deep breath that is like a long sigh of pleasure and anticipation, we realize that we have arrived.

Challenges arise—not the least of which is the challenge to be present at every moment in this new place. A few seconds ago, it seems, we were at home, and in another few seconds, we will be back there. But now, we are fully here.

We remember that ancient nomads, moving from one verdant meadow to another, carried their homes on the backs of their pack animals. Where they stopped and pitched their tents was the place they called home.

Long caravans crossing the stretches of Africa and Asia to conduct commerce in faraway lands also took their homes along with them. All of daily life went on as they proceeded from one place to another. Young people fell in love and married. Children were conceived and born. Old people died and were buried. Domestic dramas played out in all their richness. The journey was home, and home was the journey.

When we go out on the journey, we leave home, and yet, in a mysterious way, we take home with us. We may take ourselves away from home, but we do not completely forget about it.

Knowing that, we nevertheless strive with awareness to welcome the next new experience. We do not allow memories of home—or the "home" within us—to intrude upon what may be waiting for us just around the corner in this fresh place.

If our plate is full—full of thoughts of the home we left behind—there will be no room for new and delectable surprises, for the novel tastes and aromas we find in this place. We cannot receive nourishment if we are not open to it.

And so we consciously make room on our plate. We visualize how this place is serving us knowledge about others and about ourselves.

We make ourselves present for this experience.

We understand that all of the pieces of this new puzzle soon will be added to the complete picture of who we are. And where we have been, what we have done, and what we have been in this place far from home, finally, will be a part of what we know as home.

We leave home behind to collect a newer and fuller definition of home. Home is where we are now.

Sketching from Life

You do not have to be an artist to perform this grounding and awareness-engendering activity.

Several years ago, while paging through some eighteenth- and nineteenth-century travel diaries, I was struck by two themes, both having to do with drawing. The first was that the writers of the diaries invariably illustrated their text with little sketches, which were then engraved and included in the published books.

The second theme was that the authors always apologized for their sketches, calling them unprofessional, crude, and amateurish. I appreciated their candor—and noted that "amateur" comes from the Latin root *amo*, "to love." These small, delicate drawings were made not by trained artists, but by people who loved to travel and who loved to tell, and show, other people about where they had been.

Since then, I have been sketching from life while on my trips. I find that it settles me down, anchors me to the place for some time, and, in general, provides some well-needed grounding.

My first attempts at sketching what I was seeing were quite awkward—"amateurish" would be a charitable description. But, to my surprise, the more I sketched, the more I improved.

Taking a cue from those old travel diaries, I concentrated first on trying to illustrate simple architectural details. From my window in a second-floor hotel room in Siena, I drew what I saw across a narrow alley: a door with an arch over it. I just set down in a sketchbook what I was observing. My finished product showed some of the door but the entire arch, which was the thing that had caught my eye.

On later trips, I found myself drawing other small architectural features: a few spokes of an iron fence in a park, a window shutter, the corner of a terra-cotta tiled roof, a lamppost. Before long, a number of small, thin sketchbooks were accumulating on my travel shelves. Between the covers were verbal and visual memories of my trips, produced by my own hand. I had made myself into a half-decent pictorial chronicler of my travels.

The results of my sketching, however, have been nothing compared to the process. Drawing details of what I am seeing on my journeys gives me

Drawing Life

In the margin of a journal page, or on a new piece of paper, try sketching an object you can see from where you are. Observe it carefully. Take your time. It does not have to be perfect. Make your drawing reflect your unique perspective.

When you have finished sketching the object, reflect for a moment on how you felt while you were doing it. Did time seem to go by more slowly or more quickly while you were concentrating on your sketching? How can you improve your sketching the next time you decide to capture an image on paper?

a much deeper appreciation of where I am. It affords me the opportunity to be reflective. And it helps me to be fully present at every step, all through a journey.

You, too, will find sketching rewarding. Even tentative, halting attempts at sketching details of what you see on your journey will reap untold rewards.

Out here, away from home, I draw what I see. Like travelers of old, I lovingly commit to paper the images of my journey. These are reports to myself, sent from new places of my heart. And they are beautiful to behold.

*To awaken quite alone in a strange town is one of the most
pleasant sensations in the world. You are surrounded
by adventure. You have no idea of what is in store for you,
but you will, if you are wise and know the art of travel,
let yourself go on the stream of the unknown.*

Freya Stark, *Baghdad Sketches*

The Metamorphosis

We are at the heart of the heart of the journey.

To reach this point has not been easy. We have had to summon our
courage and overcome our fears. We have had to prepare thoroughly and
mindfully to arrive here. We have had to leave the warm comforts of home
and surrender to the exigencies of the road.

Now the time has come for the encounter.

The approach to this place has been full of wonder and mystery. Sometimes it has been arduous. But, with courage, we have met and overcome
those obstacles. The obstacles have departed from our path, and as they
have, vistas have opened before us.

We have reached the place toward which we have been moving.

And what do we find here?

When the heroes of mythology went off on their glorious quests, they
equipped themselves with enchanted armor and charms and potions for
their eventual meeting with destiny. These served them along the way, but

as all the world's great stories make clear, something more is called for when entering the core of the experience.

At the heart of the journey, every shield and sword, every talisman and incantation, falls away. The hero is left alone and defenseless. This is the most meaningful moment of the journey. It is why the hero undertook the journey in the first place.

Now, as the hero finally reaches the point of encounter, one virtue, above all others, is necessary. That one virtue is the willingness to change. Without the willingness to change, the hero must abandon the quest—or worse, must submit to the humiliation of defeat. With this magnificent quality, however, the hero boldly proceeds with the encounter and wins the day.

And so, utterly alone, we offer ourselves completely to this transforming moment.

We take that final step inside the temple.

Now we know.

Here within the sacred walls of this place we are met with the tremendous mystery: it is *the possibility of the new.*

An ecstatic thrill runs through us and we see everything with new eyes. We understand that our willingness to change has brought us to a metamorphosis—a fundamental transformation from the lower form of the self to a higher form.

Out of the cool shadows of the temple comes a person.

Although we did not realize it, this is the person we left home and traveled so many miles to meet. Looking into the face that looms before us, we know suddenly that we were destined for this encounter at this time—in this place.

This person is like us in many ways and in other ways is quite dissimilar. The eyes that gaze into our eyes are faintly familiar—but decidedly foreign. The hair, the features, remind us of hair and features we have known—and yet are somehow different, vaguely exotic.

A smile breaks on the face of the person we are beholding. We feel accepted and included. We feel embraced. Our heart opens.

For a moment we believe that we have done nothing to earn this gracious welcome. Then the thought sweeps over us in sudden understanding, like a strong wind from the corridors of the temple: with valor we have come to this moment; with courage we have accepted the call of the journey. We have earned this prize.

Our prize is to embrace and to be embraced by the stranger.

The stranger standing before us has qualities that we have been lacking. The stranger seems to know more, to see more, to feel more, to have many more dimensions. Beauty, serenity, compassion, and wisdom emanate as in a golden aura from the stranger.

We have glimpsed this stranger through windows that opened briefly in our quiet times. Now, our senses are filled with the presence of this new person. In a flush of emotion, we feel complete.

We recognize the person. This is not a stranger at all.

We understand.
The stranger and I are one.
The stranger is me, transformed.

Reflections of Who You Are

At the center of the journey, something in you shifts.

The person you used to be seems to fall away to reveal another version of you. The person who undertook this journey and faced seemingly insurmountable obstacles on the path is transforming into a higher, more self-aware presence.

Often the shift comes from an encounter with another person—a stranger you meet by chance, or someone you knew, but now know in a different way. Sometimes it comes in the form of an unexpected incident, a synchronicity, an accident. It may also come from the sudden vision of a world we had not dreamed existed—an astonishing landscape, a breathtaking view of the sea, a dazzling city skyline at dusk, a stunning work of art, a heart-stopping sunrise over an unfamiliar horizon.

In one startling moment, you know that you are a part of something much larger and much grander than you had ever imagined. You know that the world is huge, strange, inscrutable, and magnificent. This transporting insight puts you in a different place within, and makes you a different *you*.

The transforming moment need not occur at the destination you had set out with as your goal. The encounter can burst forth suddenly and unexpectedly along the way to your destination, or on the way back home from it. It is a sacred centerpiece that can take place anywhere.

When this divine shift happens, you begin to see people in a new light.

People you encounter on your journey are often mirrors of yourself. Describing them is an excellent way to learn more about you—not just the "you" you have known, but also the "you" into which you are transforming.

On a trip, you might encounter dozens of people. Choose one or two of them—people who stand out in your mind—and write down some of the things that strike you about them: kind, a bit of a temper, wonderful laugh, serious, careful with words, entertaining, honest. Because the person you are describing is your mirror, these attributes are also yours.

This exercise is simple, but its rewards are tremendous. It gives us the opportunity to see ourselves externalized and to appreciate ourselves more than we ever have.

The stranger at the heart of my journey is me—transformed.
I have come all this way to find this new person.
At the center of my wanderings, the world is strange,
wonderful, and new. All that I see and touch now is new.

*Travel is more than the seeing of sights; it is a change
that goes on, deep and permanent, in the ideas of living.*

Miriam Beard, *Realism in Romantic Japan*

Gifting

We have recognized ourselves in the stranger. Now we move to take what
we first saw as foreign in the stranger and to make these things part of the
familiar.

When we incorporate the truths we have just discovered, we transform
ourselves. We are renewed.

But how do we accomplish this? We want somehow to merge with the
new experiences to make them truly ours. If we do not, if we are untouched
by what is all around us, we will remain the person we were when we began
our journey.

To bring about the union of the familiar and the new, unfamiliar parts of
ourselves, there must be an exchange—a giving and a receiving. We offer to
another a token of the self we knew so well—the part of us that left home
and courageously embarked upon this journey of self-discovery.

We receive from the other the new part of ourselves.

Ceremonial gift-giving among the ancients, at the state level, was ritually prescribed and incredibly extravagant. Stories of these exchanges have come to us in great detail through written and pictorial history. Mutual presentations of exotic offerings between rulers of fabled kingdoms went on for days and weeks.

When the Queen of Sheba visited King Solomon in Judea in 950 B.C., long caravans of riches and huge herds of domesticated beasts followed her. When Queen Cleopatra entered Rome in 46 B.C., more than 500 royal barges laden with the dazzling wealth of Egypt preceded her up the Tiber, pulled by hundreds of oxen.

For our ancestors, behind the grand gesture of giving and receiving lay the concept of honoring the new and unfamiliar, and paying generous tribute to it, in order to somehow merge with it. This large-scale symbolic mingling of kingdoms was designed to elevate both the giver and the receiver.

In fairy tales, the hero, upon his victorious return from his quest, is greeted by the king and awarded the hand of the princess and half the kingdom. We understand these as metaphors for union on a new and higher level, incorporating both the old and the new in one.

In the giving of gifts brought from home, we offer ourselves the possibility of personal transformation. By the same generous act, we offer the recipient of our gifts the same opportunity for personal growth.

To the other, our gift is foreign, strange, and exotic.

To us, what we may receive in return is likewise novel and unusual. Even if no token is offered us, the person we encounter may be our gift.

The hand of the princess, half the kingdom—in the merging of ourselves with the foreign, we become new.

A Token of Your Esteem

You brought gifts from home along with you on your trip. Now is the time to give them.

Some of us go on journeys with presents but forget to hand them out—or wait for what we think might be a more appropriate time. I used to return home with gifts I had spent time and effort assembling before a trip but ended up never distributing at my destination.

When do you give a gift? Not only when, but also to whom, and how? These are good questions to ask yourself now, as you pull from your suitcase the snapshots of yourself and loved ones, along with other small reminders of the place you call home.

Some years ago I was invited by the State Department to go to Brazil and give a series of talks on the American cinema. I was living in Washington, D.C., at the time. When I packed my bags, I folded in a T-shirt I had bought at the Jefferson Memorial—on the back was a picture of the Memorial framed by a branch of cherry blossoms. The shirt, with its symbol of the nation's capital, would be a gift for someone I was yet to meet.

Every morning when I took clothes out of my suitcase and saw the shirt, I wondered who would become its owner, and when. My lecture tour was about to end and I still had not given my gift away. Hours before I was to return home, a schoolteacher came to the hotel to thank me for a presentation I had made the previous night at the Embassy. She brought with her one of her young students who was interested in film. I asked the boy the name of his school, and he answered, "Thomas Jefferson Secondary School."

"Wait here," I said, and returned a few minutes later with the shirt. The faces of both student and teacher lit up—it was as if I had planned this gift far in advance. The boy pulled the shirt on immediately, talking about how he would be the envy of his entire school.

After many years, he and I have kept in touch with each other. Every Christmas, I receive pictures of him and his wife and their children. Now we have begun communicating regularly through email. A simple gift that I had picked up almost absentmindedly became for me the door to an enriching lifelong friendship.

In matters of gift-giving, I have learned that the heart knows better than the head. There is something false in trying to rationally decide who will receive your gift or when you should give it. The heart seems to know the answer to those questions. My advice is to go with your heart.

A little courage may be necessary here. You may be shy, or just a bit reserved. If so, you are not in the habit of reaching out to new people, especially with your heart.

But you have undertaken this trip with courage; you have come boldly here, to the heart of your journey. Surely you can offer a simple gift to a new acquaintance.

See yourself offering your gift from home—a token of your esteem for the receiver. See the person accepting it graciously, regarding it with respect and gratitude.

Remember that in giving a small gift to someone new, you are doing what you came here to do. The "new person" is a mirror of yourself. You are completing your journey of self-discovery.

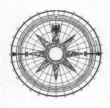

Giving of myself is a surrender of the past. Accepting the new is why I have made this glorious journey. I take one step away from myself, and I am in a new world. But no, this is the same world: I am new.

Travel broadens perspectives and teaches new ways to measure quality of life. Many travelers toss aside their hometown blinders. Their prized souvenirs are the strands of different cultures they decide to knit into their own character.

Rick Steves, *Europe Through the Back Door*

Collecting Mementos

Even in this blissful moment of encounter and exchange, our minds race ahead and race back.

Both ahead of us and behind us is home.

We are at the midpoint of the journey. From here, we start back again. And so our thoughts are of home: the home we came from, which carries our past identity, and the home we are going back to, which will be changed because we are changed.

While the fire at the center of this experience still burns brightly, we are drawn to look for something to take away from here. The prospect of returning home empty-handed is unthinkable. We need to recover a tangible reminder of this place.

We search for the mementos that will recall this enchanted time long into the future.

When Christopher Columbus returned from his first voyage of discovery in the New World, he brought back to his patron, Queen Isabella of Spain, "the treasures of the Indies"—gold and other precious minerals, parrots, exotic animals, wood, maize, sweet potatoes, plantains, and pineapples. If anyone doubted that Columbus had found an entirely new land, here was proof positive.

Each gift he presented at court carried the texture and scent of its place of origin. These mementos were pieces of the great mosaic of world discovery. For Columbus, they were a remembrance of the fascinating lands he had so recently trod; for the spellbound Isabella, they were the distilled essence of the lands themselves.

History records that in the year following the first triumphal homecoming of Columbus, court doctors in Spain used an assortment of peppers brought back from the New World, unknown in Europe at that time, to treat an ailing Isabella. Symbolically, "the new" was used to regenerate "the old"—and a memento from the epic journey was the medium of the healing.

We search for a similar tangible remembrance of this place—a relic from here that will have a special meaning for us. We look for something that epitomizes the stage upon which we have acted out our transformation.

This search for something of value to our hearts is a quest-within-a-quest. It is the journey in microcosm.

Seeking the perfect memento, finding it, bringing it back—this is the very essence of the journey. We undertake it with care, with awareness.

The prized souvenir we pack away to bring back is incontrovertible proof that we have discovered our own New World.

A Recollection of the Journey

I used to regard souvenirs as a necessary bother. They were part of the un-avoidable obligations of travel. Most of the time I thought of them at the last minute—usually as presents for family and friends back at home.

Lately, though, I have been seeing the wisdom of choosing appropriate mementos of a journey. Now they have become for me reminders of where I have been—both in the literal and the figurative sense.

You will find that mindful selection and taking back of mementos will add immeasurably to the experience of your journey.

Every small memento from a trip is a recollection of the journey in tangible form. At the time you buy a souvenir, or are given a token of remembrance, it may seem insignificant. Once you are home, however, the small item will expand into something much larger in your mind and your heart.

Since everyone has a different experience of a journey, everyone will take away from that experience something entirely different. The things you are given on a trip or things you buy to take back home will be completely un-like anyone else's remembrances. That is what makes them so special.

On a book tour once I found myself in Washington, D.C., in autumn. Any-one who lives there or has visited there at that time of the year will know the beauty of the big, colorful fall leaves. Early one morning I left the small hotel where I was staying and walked through the back streets of Georgetown. The pavement was strewn with leaves blown from trees the rainy night before. Or-anges, yellows, brilliant reds all formed a magnificent mosaic at my feet.

I knelt down and collected some of the leaves—a few of each color. To a passerby I must have looked peculiar, indeed. But I tucked those leaves away and pressed them in a favorite book, where they still live, reminding me of that day and that time in my life.

You will want to look for something that also has a powerful meaning for you—something that will recall a transformative aspect of the trip. It may be something as simple as the menu from a café where you met someone who has become important to you. Or it could be a pass to a museum or a performance where you received a significant insight.

The Road Traveled

Complete these sentences:

"The most surprising thing I am finding out about myself is . . ."

"What I am learning about other people that I never knew before is . . ."

"Among the spiritual provisions I brought with me on this journey, I should have included . . ."

"If I had more time to spend at my destination, I would have . . ."

"Because of what I am discovering about myself and others, I may have to adjust my thinking, in this way . . ."

End your journal entry with gratitude to yourself for having heeded the call to journey and having answered it with such dedication.

Forget buying something expensive. I have never found the most important mementos to have anything to do with cost. They are not for impressing people back home with a fancy price tag. They are for making you aware of the journey as an inner experience.

Choosing mementos in this way, you may even come up with souvenirs that you had thought trite—a paperweight of the Empire State Building or a glass snow-globe of the Eiffel Tower. What might be a cliché in another context might be just the right memento, personally, for you to take back home.

You will find that the simplest things will create an enormous impact upon your return.

I collect evidence of my travels. When I end this journey, I will have these things to remind me that I was courageous— that I did not shrink from change. These tokens are the proof of my transformation. Now I am ready to return from whence I came.

Part Four

The Homecoming

He who returns from a journey
is not the same as he who left.

Chinese Proverb

The pleasure of leaving home, care-free, with no concern but to enjoy, has also as a pendant the pleasure of coming back to the old hearthstone, the home to which, however traveled, the heart still fondly turns, ignoring the burden of its anxieties and cares.

Herman Melville, "Traveling"
in *The Piazza Tales and Other Prose Pieces*

The hero's return home from the adventures of the road is one of the great themes running through all mythology.

In our time, we give scant attention to the process of homecoming. Often, we are in a hurry to go back home from the place we designated as the destination of our journey. Thinking that the destination is the entire purpose of the journey, we quit that place and hasten to where we started out, as if this period were a kind of limbo between our exhilarating exploration out in the world and the safe harbor at journey's end.

But in ancient times, that was not the case. Odysseus took ten years to return home from the Trojan War. During that time, he experienced amazing adventures and grew in strength and wisdom. As chronicled by Homer in the *Odyssey*, the end of the war was just the beginning of the long and exciting homecoming for the hero. By the time he finally arrived back at his kingdom in Ithaca, he was transformed by a long list of heroic exploits—he was a different person from the one who left Troy bound for home.

Orpheus descended into the Underworld to retrieve his beloved Eurydice, but it was only on the way home from that shadowy place that the most important event of the journey occurred. The hero was told that he could bring Eurydice into the world above, but only on the condition that he not look back. Unfortunately, nearing the mouth of the cave that led out to the light, Orpheus glanced over his shoulder to see whether his sweetheart was following, and at that moment she receded into the darkness.

The way home for Theseus is the most significant part of his journey out of the maze of the Labyrinth. He has slain the Minotaur, but now he must wind up the string Ariadne has given him and with which he has traced his trail to find the monster. If he cannot find his way home, all is lost.

On his way back from the heroic feat of decapitating Medusa, Perseus finds the beautiful Andromeda chained to a rock, waiting to be sacrificed to a sea serpent. Perseus falls in love with her and, when the serpent rises out of the sea to claim its victim, he kills it. He leaves with Andromeda and returns to his island home. The homeward journey held not only adventure, but also undying love for the hero.

In the same way, we can connect with the archetype of the voyage home to understand more about our own travels and other experiences that are our life's journeys. By keeping our eyes open and our wits about us as we return from an encounter, we can be given the gift of a deeper self-discovery.

On a plane on her way home from a disastrous business trip, during which her world virtually fell apart, a young woman buries herself in a book. The elderly woman next to her finally gets her attention and asks a favor: she is going to visit her estranged sister, to make amends after years of conflict, and needs the younger woman's help with making connections, recovering her baggage, and finding transportation into the city. Suddenly the young woman, who thought of herself as a failure, becomes someone's caregiver and protector; her life has a new meaning. This incident, which elevates the way she sees herself in the world, happens on the way back from what the woman thought was the purpose of her trip.

When the heroes returned home, their first task was to reorder their kingdom. Odysseus, back at Ithaca, finds his palace in disrepair and his wife being courted by greedy suitors. He sends the suitors packing—some to their eternal rewards—and begins to reorder everything under his domain.

Our task upon our return from a journey is to reorder our lives around our new identity. The encounter, whether it arose at our destination or on the way to it, or on the way home from it, has transformed us. Now our work is to change our world to accommodate our enlarged identity. This is a sacred undertaking. It acknowledges the altering effects of the journey. Coming home, we are different somehow—and our world needs to reflect the new person.

Odysseus, once at home, reshapes his kingdom, restores his son to his rightful position, and recovers his loving wife, Penelope. The hero, back at home, creates a new harmony for himself and for everyone in the kingdom.

Establishing this new harmonious balance to our lives after being out in the world is essential to the arc of the journey. The myths reinforce this new spiritual equilibrium. In her book, *Mythology,* Edith Hamilton ends her section about the epic adventures of Odysseus on this lyrical note: "Gaily they trod a measure, men and fair-robed women, till the great house around them rang with their footfalls. For Odysseus at last after long wandering had come home and every heart was glad."

To leave is to die a little,
To die to what we love.
We leave behind a bit of ourselves
Wherever we have been.

Edmond Haraucourt, *Choix de Poésies*

Leaving for Home

Getting to this place required much effort; adapting to it took courage and patience. Now we don't want to leave.

The pain of separation is much like what we experienced as we left home. In a strange way, this place has become home.

And now we feel the stirrings of other apprehensions. Questions begin to occupy our thoughts: What will life be like away from here? What will we find when we go back to the place we originally left?

It has been said that we die a little when we leave a place. And so it is.

The prelude to homecoming involves completing and concluding all that this place has meant to us. While we draw all the strands of this place together, we reflect on the fabric of our traveling, a perfect tapestry, which we are weaving with our many experiences. We are seeing the end of things here. We are sensing fullness and satisfaction—consummation.

The arc of our journey now begins to descend, like the sun passing mid-day. In the golden light of our last moments here, we recollect and we imagine our next steps into the future.

Finding the way back home from a quest is a common theme in all great literature. Getting back from the place that once was our destination is as important as getting to it—and just as filled with meaning for us.

Finding our way back home is significant. And once we depart we are not to look back.

Ariadne's thread, critical for Theseus to find his way out of the Labryinth and the theme of our journey, is our lifeline home. To return safely from this place, we must be aware of why we came here and what we accomplished. The thread that runs throughout this trip must be acknowledged. Our conscious leaving will assure that we go home triumphant and fully satisfied.

The admonition the gods gave to Orpheus rings in our imagination: "Do not look back!" We are to close this chapter of the journey and close it firmly. To wonder whether we truly completed all we came here to do, to imagine for a moment that we have left the journey somehow undone, would show a lack of faith in our gods of travel.

Memories—oh, yes. We will be looking back in that way when, home at last, we sort through the treasures of the place we have been.

We depart now, with respect, affection, and gratitude, laden with our experiences of self-discovery.

We depart.

Reflecting on the Place

With a few homemade ceremonies, you can make your departure one of the most important phases of your journey.

Often you are not even given the opportunity to reflect on the place you are leaving or on the wonderful things that happened there. In the commotion of packing, arranging transportation, and attending to other details, you might forget a ritual that can put the entire journey into perspective.

On the day before my departure, I always leave two or three hours to be by myself. Alone, I feel the pangs of leaving and the swelling of gratitude for having been here. Awash in these feelings, I perform three ceremonies.

I share these with you to try if you wish, or adapt them to suit your needs.

First, revisit two or three specific locations that have become important

Expectations

Think for a moment about where you have been. Was it all you had imagined it would be before you set out on your journey? How was it different from what you had expected? How was it the same as you had pictured at the start of your journey?

List five expectations you had about your journey before leaving home. Next to them, write down how those expectations might have changed—or remained the same—as you lived through the stages of your journey.

to you—an outdoor café where you had coffee every morning, a bridge where you watched sailboats float lazily below, an isolated stretch of beach, a hillside carpeted in wildflowers. Consciously say good-bye. If you feel comfortable doing it, you can say good-bye aloud and thank the place.

Second, choose one of the locations and, in your journal of feelings, write a simple good-bye note to it (and, by extension, to all your locations): "Farewell—and thank you for all you have given me!"

Finally, as you leave the place where you have been staying, bless it for the next person. You have the power to bless—and this is one of the best ways to use that power.

I depart this place that has given me so much. I express my affection and my gratitude for the insights it has provided me.
Before I go, perhaps never to return, I leave my blessing. May all who come here be healed, as I have, in the discovery of their true selves.

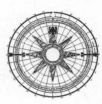

Only that traveling is good which reveals to me the value of home and enables me to enjoy it better.

Henry David Thoreau, *Journal*

The Return

We are home!

We return with a full heart. We come home carrying with us the prize from the quest, the promise of a bright future.

While on the journey, from time to time we revisited this place in our mind. During a lull in our adventures, we wandered back here and, in our imagination, walked among these rooms, so filled with meaning, so imbued with our spirit.

Now we are back, and what we left behind glows brighter, greets us, and welcomes us. We went forth from this place with hope. We return to it with a treasure of experiences and with a new knowledge of ourselves.

This new knowledge continues to unfold.

While out in the world, away from here, we have not been idle. We have successfully met the challenges presented by new places and new people.

These encounters have made us stronger and wiser.

We return joyful, energetic, prepared to accept new ways of seeing others—and ourselves.

This, the return home, is also part of the journey. Making our way back mindfully connects us with the universal idea of homecoming.

In ancient Rome, when generals returned home from a victorious campaign, they camped outside the city for days, sometimes weeks, as a grand entrance was planned and a triumphal arch was constructed. Finally, after prodigious and meticulous preparation, they began the parade into the heart of Rome. Long carts filled with the spoils of war, with exotic animals, with captive enemy officers, preceded the conquering general, who rode in a golden chariot drawn by white steeds.

Those glorious entries into the Forum became the stuff of legend, celebrated in historical accounts and still visible on the carved columns and temple walls of modern Rome.

We also return triumphant, with new self-knowledge born in other places.

Another universal idea emerges: putting the household back in order. What we find upon our arrival may not be the same place that we left. If the order of the home is the metaphor for the way we were before we embarked on the journey, then some modifications may be necessary—for we ourselves have changed in the time we were away.

Odysseus comes home to Ithaca after a twenty-year absence—ten of it spent in mortal combat in Troy and another ten engaged in amazing adventures on the long voyage back. His kingdom is in disarray. His estates are in ruin, his lands are lying fallow, and his beloved wife is being courted by a score of brutish suitors.

Quickly, with the strength and wisdom gained on his epic journey, he rids the kingdom of the encroachers and decrees the restoration of his houses and the planting of his fields.

Now, truly, he is home.

And so we return. We reenter our home in triumph. We set everything in order.

Slowly, as we rest in this new place, which is the old place transformed, we feel the immensity of what we have undertaken and accomplished, and we are warmed at this familiar, embracing hearth.

Your Triumphal Arch

I never paid much attention to entering my house when I returned from a trip. Coming home was about getting in the door, putting my bags down, and sinking into an easy chair.

But lately I have made much more of my return—and it has served to make my entire journey a richer, more conscious experience.

You, too, can make a ritual entrance into your home.

When you left on your trip, the last act you performed on the way out of the house—both in a literal and figurative sense—was closing the door. You may have made a little ceremony of it by closing the door behind you slowly and with awareness of your leave-taking.

Coming home presents the opportunity for doing the same, but in reverse. Before entering the house, stand outside for a moment, remember that you are still "away from home," then open the door and step inside.

Crossing the threshold is an act of momentous importance. A moment ago you were still on the road, still a traveler. Now, in the next moment, you are across the line, back home. The doorway is your triumphal arch.

You close the door behind you with the same intense clarity that accompanied you when you left on your trip. You are inside.

You are home.

If you listen carefully—before you survey the rooms, before you open your mail, before you check the messages on your phone and on your computer—you will hear the cheering of the crowds as you enter your domain in triumph.

In the land of the stranger I encountered the monsters of self-doubt, fear, and limitation. I met them on the field and won the day.
Now I return triumphantly in a chariot of gold.
I enter the city of my birth crowned with laurel. I am home.

*If we are always arriving and departing, it is also
true that we are eternally anchored. One's destination is
never a place, but rather a new way of looking at things.*

Henry Miller, *Big Sur and the Oranges of Hieronymus Bosch*

To Honor the Adventure

We have come home.

It is cause for celebration!

But for just this short period, we remain quiet and reflective. Our celebration is an interior one—no less joyous than an outward observance with family and loved ones. Now we crave stillness to process where we have been and what we have done—to honor the adventure.

Later we will announce our homecoming. We will reveal ourselves to the people in our lives. We will show them what we have brought back from our travels. At this moment, however, we are alone, assimilating our experiences and basking in the accomplishment of the journey.

Slowly, we make a much smaller excursion—this one around the very home that we left. We visit the four corners of this world, one by one. It has diminished in size somewhat. It is smaller than we remembered.

Or have we somehow gotten larger?

They are still here, these things we left behind. An article of clothing, eliminated from the packing process, lies on the bed. A half cup of coffee sits on the counter. And, on the table, spread open to a favorite section, is the morning newspaper of the day we embarked on our journey.

Suddenly we begin to see everything around us in a new way.

All of this represents the old. But we are not the same as we were when we last handled these things. We have been transformed by the journey. We have encountered "the other"—our mirror image—and that meeting has made us stronger, wiser, and more whole.

The hero enters the city in triumph, and all that was left behind at home is charged with the new radiance of personal transformation.

We come home, having braved the world away from here, bringing back the knowledge of self that will make our lives fuller and more compassionate.

We acknowledge and honor the old—all that was here when we left home. And we welcome in the new.

All of it is good.

For we realize that nothing we see, nothing we hear or feel, has a meaning beyond us. All simply is. Our conscious awareness bestows definition to everything in our world.

Alone, we wander through this microcosm of our universe, accustoming ourselves to it again.

The adventure of exploration and discovery has almost reached its glorious conclusion. Tomorrow we will tie all the ends of this amazing tapestry together. Today we sit quietly, still weaving those threads, regarding with wonder all that has been altered—upward—by our journey.

Offerings

One of the most glorious moments in your journey comes when you have arrived home, entered the house, and closed the door behind you.

Your trip is over, but your journey is not.

You can give this moment a spiritual meaning with a simple ritual that goes back in antiquity to the epic travelers of history and myth. This is an extraordinary time—and savoring it and celebrating it will add to the closure of your trip.

A few years ago, after I began making travel shrines for each of my journeys, I stumbled upon a meaningful ceremony that I now perform as an indispensable part of my return home.

If you read the great stories of world literature, you see that heroes, on their return from a great quest, often make their first visit to the temple of the god or goddess who protected them through their journey. Symbolically, they acknowledge divine assistance in undertaking and completing their adventures.

They approach the temple altar, say a few words of thanksgiving, and place upon it a libation of wine and a dish of delicacies—figs, dates, nuts, and other treats. Offering these tokens to the deities is the hero's way of paying tribute to the powerful spiritual forces that guided him on the road and brought him back safely home.

I perform the same ceremony at my travel shrine—and I do it literally. I pour out a small bowl of wine, prepare a dish of sweets, and place them on my altar. These living items—representing not only sustenance, but also opulence—sitting there among the other emblems and mementos of my journey, lend a vital new energy to the entire shrine.

Other ritual offering possibilities: flowers, coins, incense, candles. The gods of travel love light and water. Lighting a candle upon your return and keeping a small bowl of water on your altar are excellent ways of attracting the good energy of the journey and honoring all it has done for you while you were away.

When you offer your token delicacies to the gods of your shrine—whether they are wine and dried fruits as in ancient times or your own modern counterpart—remember to sing out your hero's jubilant song: "I celebrate the new; I honor the old. I give thanks for the end of the journey!"

At the altar of my epic journey, I offer gratitude to the powers that have impelled me to self-discovery. For me, as for the heroes of old, the journey draws to a close in thanksgiving. In the temple of this journey to the heart of myself, I bask in the light of new wisdom so dearly won, so graciously given.

Once you have traveled, the voyage never ends, but is
played out over and over again in the quietest chambers.
The mind can never break off from the journey.

Pat Conroy

The New Order of Things

Now, to adjust to what we have found upon our return.

Things are different. No, things are the same—we are different. We notice subtle changes, quiet shifts of energy. At home, we seem to see more; at work, we undertake old tasks with more detachment.

The journey has brought about a new order of things.

We are no longer the same as we were when we left home. Finding who we are now, and arranging everything in our world around that new definition, is our challenge.

In fairy tales, the main character often undergoes a profound change at the end of an adventure. A frog is turned into a knight. A pauper reveals himself to be a prince.

Before life can be lived "happily ever after," a fundamental change must take place.

Ovid's *Metamorphoses* takes its name from the poet's stories of change. In one, the sculptor Pygmalion falls in love with his own creation, a life-sized statue of a beautiful woman. From Mt. Olympus, Venus takes pity on the artist and transforms the statue into a living woman, Galatea.

In another of Ovid's stories, the beautiful Daphne, fleeing the advances of the god Apollo, runs for help to her father, a river deity. When she reaches the bank of the river, her father hears her plea, and she is changed into a laurel tree—which forever afterward is sacred to the worship of Apollo.

Personal transformation is a theme throughout world literature. People are turned into stone or into pillars of salt as punishment; they become trees, birds, rivers, and flowers as rewards for good deeds. Always, the change is a lesson.

We, too, are transformed by our recent experiences away from home. Now, as a new routine begins to emerge in our daily life, we start to see the many sides of our personal metamorphosis. And it delights us.

The change that has come upon us is growth.

Everything in our world now needs to be evaluated to see whether it fits with the new person we have become. This is a time of observing, analyzing, weighing, and imagining alternatives.

Perhaps the greatest gift of the journey is the awareness that we have the power to re-create our lives. Such is the magic of travel! We have been changed by our experiences on the journey. Now, the legacy of the journey is the power to assume an active role in our growth.

Travel transformed us; now we transform ourselves.

We do it by instituting a new order in our world. The new world around us conforms to who we truly are now.

A Taoist saying tells us, "The journey is the reward."

Suddenly, we comprehend all that is being said in these rich words of wisdom. The gift of the journey is nothing less than a new world of our own creating.

Create Your New World

Returning from your adventure, you can re-invent yourself and re-create your world.

A drawing or collage suggestion: Using crayons, colored pens, pencils, magazine clippings, scissors, and paste, create a new landscape for your transformed self.

This is a fun exercise, but it is also a serious way of actually visualizing how you can wrap a completely new world around yourself—a world that conforms to and supports the new person you have become during your travels.

Picture yourself in your new world, and then depict the people, the places, and the things that bring meaning to the new you.

The Power to Transform

You can do something simple and symbolic to lock in your acknowledgment that everything has changed—and that you have the power to transform your world.

Now that you are back from your journey, you can refashion everything around you. The truth is, you not only have the ability to change things, but you also have the obligation to do so.

Some people, when this realization sweeps over them, reorganize their lives in ways they never would have imagined before leaving on a trip. I have seen friends do everything from rearranging the living room furniture to quitting a boring job. Travel had an impact on them that remained after they returned home and impelled them to take some transformational action.

You do not have to go as far as getting into a new line of work to change things in your world after a journey—although that certainly may be an option. Most people find that they return to both home and the workplace with so many fresh ideas and novel approaches that life may seem to be an entirely new experience.

Here is a small but effective activity that will signal your power to create a new order of things. Find something that you used almost every day before your journey—a favorite coffee mug, an article of clothing—such as a sweater or slippers—a familiar piece of recorded music, a particular scented soap or shampoo.

Take this symbol of the "old order" of your life, put it away in a closet, and replace it with a new version—preferably something you may have brought back with you from your travels.

This small, conscious re-creation of a part of your world registers on the unconscious as a powerful act of self-transformation. Other, larger changes will follow.

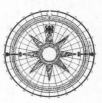

The journey has given me the power to change my world. I take that power in my hands and, like the magician that I am, transform everything around me. In this way, I make my world conform to the new person that is my discovered self.

And the end of all our exploring
Will be to arrive where we started
And know the place for the first time.

T. S. Eliot, "Little Gidding"

Completing the Circle of the Journey

We close the circle of travel that began so long ago with our leave-taking. We know that marking the end of travel is as important as acknowledging the start of it.

With awareness, we draw the circle up.

Now is the time for reviewing and planning. This is the moment of insight—of hindsight and foresight.

The angel of the journey spoke to us in a dream, saying, "Go forth!" We heard the distant call of travel and entertained the possibility of change. To leave home and venture out on the road would take courage, which we summoned toward the promise of a significant encounter.

Flush with anticipation, we closed the door upon the past. We brought with us fortitude, patience, perseverance, valor—our spiritual provisions.

The path to the destination was not easy—setting out in the great unknown never is easy. Thorns of discord were strewn about on the road; un-expected emotional ruts pitted the trail. And sometimes fear haunted us.

At last we arrived at the new place.

Shakespeare tells us "journeys end in lovers meeting." This journey cul-minated in an encounter that changed us to our very heart. Truly, lovers met. We have seen ourselves in the mirror of the other, and we have been transmuted at the sight.

Leaving the new land was as difficult as leaving home had been. In a strange, mystical way, that place had become home—for, indeed, it was "home" to the emerging of our newly transformed self.

We gathered mementos—relics of the journey. These precious, mute ob-jects would tell the tale.

And suddenly, perhaps all too soon, we were finding our way back along the road toward home. Again the path was uneven and arduous. But this time we had the advantage of familiarity, and, like Theseus, the thread of the journey—its special theme—to guide and comfort us.

"Where we love is home," says the poet Oliver Wendell Holmes in "Homesick for Heaven." "Home that our feet may leave, but not our heart."

We walk from room to room in this place that is as well known to us as the contours of our own face. Here is where we lately spent so much time, laughed with family and friends, loved, wept, celebrated, pondered, and planned our life. It is rich with the shadows of our comings and goings.

But we have changed. Now we alter this environment, which is the abode of "the old," to fit the new person we have become. We re-create our world, as we have re-created ourselves. And thus we bring the journey to a close.

The covenant we made with our angel of travel in those days long ago is now fulfilled.

We rest in the satisfaction of having found the courage required for this adventure. All around, this new world of our own making comforts us.

In the silence, the Voice comes to us: every journey is a journey inward. Travel in the outer world is a metaphor for the inner journey.

And the end of the journey is transformation.

A Sacred Event

If you created a shrine to your journey, now is the time to dismantle it. Do it with a sense of ceremony, and you will elevate the conclusion of your trip to a sacred event.

Even if you did not create a travel shrine, you can make a ritual of putting away the things you have brought back with you.

Journey's end is a time for reflection and celebration. Closure is one of the most important aspects of a trip. Leaving a journey open-ended is tantamount to not completing a delicious meal with dessert or not finishing a really good book. Ending a trip properly brings enormous satisfaction.

The literature of travel is full of references to the ends of journeys: the leprechaun finally finds the pot of gold at the end of the rainbow (a metaphor for the arc of the journey of life); the hero is crowned with a wreath of laurel leaves (sacred to Apollo, god of the sun, which travels the sky every day); lovers finally kiss at the end of the movie (a symbol for integration—transformation in union).

In the great myths, journey's end is marked by celebrations, reunions, and completions. Odysseus is reunited with his beloved, long-suffering Penelope; Theseus comes home to his new bride, gentle Ariadne; Perseus and Andromeda, in the words of Edith Hamilton, "live happily every after." Aeneas ends his heroic journey on the banks of the Tiber River, where he and the beautiful Lavinia found the race of noble Romans that go on to change the world.

By the end of a trip, your travel shrine has accumulated an assortment of meaningful objects. It holds pre-trip tokens such as travel brochures, itineraries, and pictures of family, friends, and animal companions, which you left here for symbolic safekeeping while you traveled. In with those are post-trip souvenirs such as ticket stubs, menus, postcards, trinkets, snapshots, and small rocks or pieces of driftwood.

Your shrine also holds your Fear Box—that little box into which you placed only your rational fears before you left home.

The first part of the ceremony: Take the slips of paper that contain your fears and burn them in a ritual dish or pot. The journey is over, and so are the apprehensions that may have threatened to steer you away from your path.

Next, put away almost all of the keepsakes on your altar or your travel shrine. Hold back one or two things to remind you of the journey, and place them where you will see them every day.

Finally, lovingly, take the shrine down.

My journey is over, but my discovery of myself is only beginning. I am at peace.

Part Five

Recounting the Tale

*The hero of my tale, whom I love with all
the power of my soul, whom I have tried
to portray in all his beauty, who has been,
is, and will be beautiful, is Truth.*

Leo Tolstoy

Do not go where the path may lead; go instead where there is no path and leave a trail.

Ralph Waldo Emerson

After the homecoming, the journey appears to be over. But the circle of our expedition of the spirit is not closed until we report what we have discovered and revealed what we have brought back with us.

In the ancient myths, the hero returns home in triumph. A sumptuous banquet is prepared to honor the traveler. During the banquet the hero stands and recounts the tale of the adventure. Engrossed in the story, everyone in the banquet hall is transported in imagination to those distant lands the hero so recently toured—and returned alive to tell about.

This is the moment when the hero ceases being the traveler and assumes the mantle of teacher.

When we at last leave the rigors of the road and come home to reflect on the lessons we have learned "out there," it is time to give to others the benefits of our new knowledge. This is not a dispensable appendage to the journey—it is an integral part of the experience, without which our adventures would be open-ended and unfinished. All the world waits breathless for what we have to say about the interior landscape we have explored, and the insight we have gained in the process.

Perseus, after slaying Medusa, begins the long voyage home. On the way back home he has another adventure, rescuing the beautiful Andromeda, who becomes his lover. This would be enough for any hero, but the epic journey of Perseus is not over. He returns to the kingdom of Polydectes, the man he had sought to impress with his boast to find and kill the monster. But at home, things have changed. His mother has refused marriage to King Polydectes and has gone into hiding to avoid his royal wrath. Now Polydectes is the young hero's enemy.

The already eventful journey of Perseus would seem to be over as soon as he weighs anchor at the island kingdom of Polydectes. He has returned with the head of Medusa and with a new bride. But his journey is far from over. Now he needs to recover his mother from her hiding place and then move against the cruel king.

He finds his mother and is reunited with her, and then he makes for the palace of King Polydectes. A banquet is in progress. Immediately, while all eyes are upon him, he heaves Medusa's head from his bag and Polydectes and everyone else in the hall are at once turned to stone.

Just when we think our journey is over, the last piece of business appears on the horizon. By exhibiting his dreadful trophy to Polydectes and the court assembled in the banquet hall, Perseus presents the evidence of his courage, daring, and ingenuity. The snaky head proves that he has left home, has engaged the demon, and has returned. It is the lesson of the journey, so powerful that the sight of it literally paralyzes those who behold it.

When we return from our travels, we display the evidence of our venturing forth, and it is a lesson to those who stayed at home. If we have not shared the story of our wanderings and what we learned from them, we have not completed the epic round of the adventure. Closing the circle by relating the tale ends the journey and redefines us—hero, still, but now a person who is qualified to share what we have learned with others. Our bold traverse of the world outside has won us the right to teach.

The epic cycle of the mythic journey comes to rest in this final phase. We must end the journey for another reason. Life is an upward spiral of consciousness, always in the process of unfolding. If we never come in from the road, we cannot venture forth again. Ending the journey offers us the opportunity of repose and retreat—but much more, it allows us to become the traveler again. When the urge to leave home and go out into the world, the call to journey, comes again, we can be ready to undertake a fresh new adventure.

This seeming lull is vital to the rhythm of life. We need time to be at home, to make our nest in this place of quiet emotions and serene thoughts. Time to collect, time to absorb—and time to grow, but slowly and in the shade.

And out of this blessed time, we open ourselves again to the possibility of becoming the traveler, off on another mighty quest of self-discovery.

*I may not have gone where I intended to go, but I think
I have ended up where I intended to be.*

Douglas Adams

Assembling the Threads of the Journey

As a new routine at home and at work begins to set in, we ask, what has happened? Where have we been?

Something wonderful has happened. We have been on a journey of exploration and discovery that has led us back to the heart of ourselves.

Now, in the comforts of home, in the warmth of the blazing hearth, we prepare to tell the tale of our wanderings. This has been our own epic expedition, and it has been filled with amazing adventures.

We gather together the errant corners of our story.

It may be that someone who hears our tale will decide upon a change of course by the example of our experience. Perhaps a prospective voyager will be able to avoid the pitfalls to which we nearly succumbed. Someone seated around the fire with us will be inspired to make a similarly brave journey.

Our tale will be like a flint that ignites the hearts of those who hear it.

The stories of the great adventures are our teachers. Heroes set off on demanding quests, perform miraculous tasks with divine assistance, and return home victorious. At the end of the journey they report back to the people who remained at home, and they reap the rewards.

We understand that these epic tales are metaphors for the upward movements of consciousness. We step into the winged sandals of the hero.

Like the hero, we started out, we accomplished, we returned. Now we are finding the thread that runs throughout and ties the tale together.

Our story is valuable, for it is the record of our self-exploration and self-discovery. And so we formulate the arc of our personal narrative. Others may find in it a route to their own salvation.

An inscription was scratched on one of the caravels of Columbus, 1492: "Following the sun, we left the old world."

Thus begins our own story.

And now we relive the chronicle, review it, and set it out. We followed the sun; we left the old world. What we found in the new world, and how we made our way back, is the stuff of our epic tale.

Your Epic Tale

You may have been keeping a "feelings journal" on this trip. This kind of writing is a record of how you felt and what was happening to you while you were traveling.

Now you may want to write something entirely different: the story of your trip as you lived it—not from the inside, as it were, but from the outside, as if you were the major character in your drama.

I stumbled upon this exercise after a trip I took with some friends and their eleven-year-old daughter. I heard the girl telling the story of her journey to one of her classmates. She treated it exactly like a fairy tale—with herself as the beautiful princess.

Since then I have returned again and again to this activity as a way of elevating my travel to the level of myth.

Writing your tale is a good way to assemble the threads of the journey. It is also one of the most important activities you can do at this stage to heighten your trip's spiritual content.

Start with a simple list of what actually happened while you were away from home. Find a quiet time. Sit down with pen and paper, or sit at your computer. Then, in chronological order as you remember them, write out a list of things that you did or that happened to you on the trip. Try not to judge your items ("I went to that museum but probably shouldn't have . . .); just jot down the facts.

When you have finished, you should have a good chronology. Now organize your list into a narrative story. Be sure to put everything into the past tense and to refer to yourself in the third person ("She did such-and-such or he said such-and-such.").

Try to use as many details as you can remember, and create vivid images of your experiences. Grammar and syntax are less important than your visceral memory of events—how you felt, what you were thinking at the time, how things looked to you, what you sensed.

After your story is complete, two things remain to be committed to paper. At the top of the page, write out the words, "Once upon a time . . ." and at the end write, ". . . lived happily ever after."

The story of your journey has now become an epic legend.

When you see the tale of your trip written out in this way, you will begin to understand it in the context of an archetype. Objectifying your journey has a way of making your personal experience seem universal. And, to be sure, it is.

You are the hero of your own story. You deserve an epic tale to document our exploits.

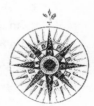

My story is the journey of my life through time and space. It is a tale of valiant undertakings—fording rushing rivers, making my way through the dark woods, crossing the long, wide fields, battling dragons—this leads me to the crystal palace of wisdom. Returned, I gather the threads of the journey. I prepare to tell my tale. And what I have to say is this: "Once upon a time . . . ."

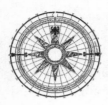

You will bring back pots and pictures. A sheaf of photographs.
A jingle of coins. But you will bring back more. A vision of a wide
world. Remembered laughter. New friends. New understanding.

Pam Brown

Displaying the Treasures

The time has come to share the treasures from our epic adventure.

All the days of the journey have led to this moment.

When we returned home, we were silent. We sat and pondered where we had been, what we had done. Events along the road were awesome, filled with wonder. Slowly, the arc of the journey began to emerge.

As the threads of the tale appeared, one by one, we gathered them and pulled them in. In time, they would come together to make the fabric of our re-created self.

We encountered the scribe within. With quill in hand, we set down our tale. As we did, the spirits of those far-off places rose up. A story glowed through. What seemed like random experiences are, we see, part of something whole. Each action helped create something full and rich.

The chronicle of the journey is a story on a grand, universal scale. It carries profound meaning not only for us, but also for everyone who is called by the gods of travel to venture forth from home.

Virgil, the celebrated court poet, stands in the midst of the banquet hall. He makes his way among the revelers reclined upon their couches, through a throng of servants hauling heaps of delicacies brought in from the far reaches of the empire. He approaches the long tables where the imperial family is assembled. His eyes meet the eyes of the emperor. It is as if he will declaim to the divine Augustus alone.

"I sing of arms and a man . . ." he begins. A hush falls over the vast room. The poet's deep, sonorous voice rings out. He launches into the thrilling tale of Aeneas, hero of the Trojan War, mythical founder of Rome.

At last he reaches the section of the tale where Aeneas and his band arrive at Carthage and are entertained at a banquet given in their honor by the resplendent Queen Dido. Aeneas, at the Queen's insistence, recites the tale of his tragic journey from Troy to the shores of Africa. "Rapt, she listened," the poet proclaims, "and the longer she heard him speak, the deeper she fell in love with him."

At the end of the end of our journey, we display our treasures. And the first of these is the story of the journey itself.

Like Virgil, we share our tale with those who assemble—loved ones who bade farewell to us when we left home, who welcomed us when we returned, and who kept us in their hearts all the time we were away. And as we tell our story, one by one the riches we brought back from our wanderings pour out.

Showing our treasures plays the journey through again. As we do, we notice that certain phases of the excursion that we might have thought insignificant come to the fore; areas of our story that we once believed to be the most consequential fade into the background.

Displaying what we have brought back is our way of making the tale more complete.

Each memento is a witness of where we have been.

And each time we bring a memento forth, what it says is, "I sing of the epic quest of bravery in the face of danger . . . of perseverance and kindness . . . of the exhilaration of self-exploration and discovery."

Share the Experience

Holding a party to talk about your trip and show what you have brought back would seem to be the easiest activity in the world. And yet, it has a deep meaning for the conscious traveler.

To approach this show-and-tell exercise with awareness, you may want to follow some simple steps.

The first involves timing. It is best to wait a few days, a week, or more before going public with your trip. The time between your homecoming and your telling of the tale is precious. During that time you will be resting, digesting, assimilating, and attaching emotional and spiritual priorities to all the things that happened while you were away from home.

When you feel you are truly ready, invite people over. You may want to do this as one big party or as several small ones. Whatever you decide, remember that it is important for you to bring complete closure to your journey by telling the story of it to others. Displaying the treasures you brought back is part of your storytelling.

Another benefit of this activity: Your friends and family members will ask you questions as you proceed through your narrative and reveal your mementos. The interest of loved ones, and their comments, will help you see what is important in the story of your trip from another's point of view.

A note of caution: You may find, as I have found, that other people are less interested in your journey than you may have imagined. This can be a crushing blow to a heart enthusiastic about sharing the splendid insights collected along the way of the traveler. But you have been transformed by your journey, and they have not. They have stayed at home. If others seem indifferent to your travels, it is not because they are unconcerned about you—it is because they have not been changed by the same experiences that changed you.

Knowing that, you offer the testimony of your explorations in the world outside. Nothing seals a journey like telling others about it, if they sincerely want to listen. And nothing will bring you more satisfaction than sharing the story of your adventures with those you love.

My journey has opened me to the most spectacular vistas of the spirit. I offer myself, transformed, to those who stayed at home, who were not able or not willing to travel with me.

In telling the tale of my travels, I am made complete.
The art of learning fundamental common values is perhaps
the greatest gain of travel to those who wish to live at ease
among their fellows.

Freya Stark, *Perseus in the Wind*

To Find What Is Important

The revelers all have gone.

Strong shafts of morning sunlight pierce the deserted banquet hall.

We walk among the tables and the couches remembering how our voices echoed in this place last night. Here is where we stood and mesmerized the imperial household with the epic tale of our wanderings.

Now we are alone.

The story of the journey plays in our mind. The reciting of it has created something new in us. In telling the tale, we have begun to see our many exploits at a distance. From time to time during our oration, we felt that all these adventures might have been happening to another person.

In truth, the journey did happen to someone else—the person we once were but are not any longer. We have transcended the details of our travels. They have served us well. But now we are seeing the larger picture.

Like the world's great symphonies, our journey has had a theme.

Telling the tale has been a way for us to find and understand that theme.

Perseus announces to his mother's prospective husband, the noble Polydectes, that he will produce the perfect wedding present: the head of the hideous Gorgon, Medusa. This will be no easy task, for anyone who looks into the face of the serpent-haired Medusa turns instantly to stone. To slay Medusa will take cunning beyond mortal ability.

The hero goes off into the dark land to seek and slay the dreaded Gorgon—this is the archetype of going within to search out our greatest fear, to confront it, and to overcome it.

Athena, goddess of wisdom, gives Perseus her own polished shield. Now he will be able to decapitate the monster without staring it in the face by using the shield as a mirror.

Heaven always offers help to the hero. Once we have decided to undertake the responsibility of re-creating ourselves, the entire universe moves to support our efforts.

For Perseus, slaying Medusa—his worst fear—was the theme of his mission. He was successful and returned to tell the tale, holding aloft the lifeless head of his fear.

Hercules, hero of heroes, is given the gargantuan assignment to perform twelve superhuman tasks. Among them is the purging of the Augean stables in a single day. The stalls hold thousands of cattle, and they have not been cleaned for years. To perform this labor, he has to divert two rivers into the stables.

Metaphorically, the hero is called upon to rid himself of negative emotions and attitudes—and to do it quickly. The task is daunting, but he is up to it because of his resoluteness and inner strength.

Each of us is the hero of our journey.

Now we assemble the chapters of our tale to find the theme. For there is a theme to our travels, as surely as there was one for Perseus and Hercules and all the other heroes. Perhaps it is not something as grand as theirs—facing and overcoming our worst fears or confronting all that we find negative within us and washing it away in a Herculean purge. Our theme may lie in a simpler register: forgiveness, closure, retribution, duty, reunion, discovery, benevolence, responsibility, connection.

We discover the theme for our journey.

This is why we left home, why we sallied forth—and why we returned.

A Simple List

A myriad of experiences, tangles of people, a legion of emotions—your trip and its aftermath have been full and exciting.

After the gatherings with family and friends, during which you told the story of the journey, you at last have the luxury of some quiet time. This is the perfect time to articulate in a word or two what the trip was all about. Coming up with a motif for your travels is an exercise in mindfulness that lifts your journey firmly onto the spiritual plane.

Try this. List the people you encountered on the trip, and next to their names, write in a word or two describing your encounter with them. Review the words you have written. Do you see a pattern, a recurring theme?

Recently a friend of mine arrived home from a trip to the town of her childhood, which she had avoided for many years because, as a child, she had not felt accepted there.

When she sat quietly and did this exercise, she found herself writing down the words "friendly" and "kind" next to people's names. The words appeared so often that she concluded—rightly—that she had made the journey to heal her relationship with her own childhood.

Her theme: Acceptance.

I am the hero of my wanderings.
I go out and come back for a reason—and that reason
is the theme of my traveling. In the theme are locked
the lessons for which my soul is yearning.

*The real voyage of discovery lies not in discovering new lands
but in seeing with new eyes.*

Marcel Proust, *Remembrance of Things Past*

The Lesson

Now that we have discovered the overriding motif of our travels, we have
the opportunity to learn the lesson that the journey offers us.

So, we ask, what is the lesson of this journey?

We ponder what the journey has taught us. On the wings of imagination,
we fly back to the first suggestion of the journey in a dream. It was there
that the seeds of change were planted.

Then the Voice said, "Go, the world awaits you. Go, and bring back what
is missing in you. Go, and you will be transformed—healed, completed."

The story is told that when Siddhattha Gotama left the beautiful palace
and parks and pavilions of his father to go on his journey of self-discovery,
his father grieved. Many years later Siddhattha returned as the Buddha. His
father, still brokenhearted, at first refused to admit him into the palace. But
then the Buddha spoke to his father about his adventures on the road, how
he attempted many different forms of asceticism and other spiritual practices to find enlightenment. Then he sat under the bodhi tree, and, finding

the stillness within, at last understood the mysteries of the universe.

When he had heard the story of his son's travels and had grasped the lesson of the journey, the Buddha's father not only embraced him with open arms, but he became one of his followers.

Now we see that the lesson of the journey was there at the beginning, in the gentle call to venture forth. But we needed to make the journey in order to own it.

Here, at the end of the end of all our wanderings, is the lesson. We have returned, victorious, with this in hand.

The lesson is that spiritual quality we did not have before the journey. It is the attribute of soul without which we faltered and floundered. In the absence of that spiritual gift, we were somehow incomplete. Now, through enormous effort, we possess it wholly, and we feel ourselves coming into the fullness of our humanity.

Every traveler brings back a different lesson.

And every traveler brings back the same lesson, which is self-discovery.

Spiritual Gains

You took spiritual provisions with you on your journey; you also accumulated spiritual gifts during the encounter and along the way home.

List some of the spiritual qualities you may have gained during the journey, or that you may have noticed emerging from a hitherto undeveloped place within.

"I now have this spiritual quality that I never had before . . ."

"I am discovering that I have a deeper understanding of this spiritual quality within me . . ."

"This is the spiritual quality, newly discovered, that I will share with those I love . . ."

Let the Journey Be Your Teacher

Once you discover the theme of your journey, it is not difficult to discover the lesson of the trip.

This exercise is an extension of the previous one. In that example, my friend was able to heal her relationship with her childhood—symbolized by the little town in which she grew up—by listing the people she had met on her trip. Next to each person's name (sometimes the person was simply "the store clerk"), she wrote down one or two words to describe her encounter with that person.

In her case, the overriding motif of the time she spent in her hometown was "acceptance." That was her theme—a surprising and most pleasing one, particularly since she had expected just the opposite. The next step was to find the lesson of the trip. It would come naturally out of the theme.

After sitting with her list and mulling it over for some time, this is what she wrote at the bottom of the page: "I have learned from this trip to accept other people, to be open to their acceptance of me, and, most of all, to accept myself . . . just as I am."

For my friend, who had felt rejection from others early in her life and had internalized those feelings of rejection, learning this lesson represented an enormous emotional and spiritual breakthrough.

Your lessons from travel will be your own. They may not always be as profound as those of my friend, but they will present themselves, if you allow them. And when they emerge, they will comfort you and heal you.

The journey is your teacher—and you have been its willing student.

The lessons of this journey will stay with you forever.

I weave out of the fabric of my wanderings a tapestry of teachings. Everywhere I have gone, everything I have done, has been for this—the spiritual lesson that I now take within. Had I stayed at home when the journey called me, I would never have learned this lesson. Gratitude fills my heart.

One could argue that a few individuals—sailors, fliers, travelers, or mountaineers—which appearing needlessly to expose themselves to danger and death may, in fact, be unconsciously serving the interest of us all. . . .

Mary Russell

The New Dream

The journey ends at the junction of another road.

And another journey begins.

Inner travel knows no dead ends, only new avenues opening onto fresh journeys.

We have told the epic tale of our mighty adventures. We have retired to this place from which we began our journey so long ago. We have come here alone to ponder the spiritual significance of our going out and coming in. The gods of travel have showered us with glorious insight, so that now we understand at last the reasons for our long sojourn in those far-off lands.

The journey has been our soul's teacher. It has taught us well; we have learned its lessons. And now we are home.

Inexorably, life proceeds. We absorbed all we have experienced, and we have been transformed by it.

The traveler who left home is not the same traveler who returned. We are different; we are new. And this newness is the higher throne from which we survey the enchanted countryside of our life.

Home.

For a moment, we believe that we will never leave here. For a moment, we imagine it would be madness to entertain abandoning the comforts of this blessed place.

Tell Your Story

We learn from the experiences of each other. When Marco Polo returned from China and told his family, then his friends, then all of Venice about what he had seen, he opened the eyes, the minds, and the hearts of everyone who heard his story. He changed history.

You have returned from your journey with your own life-changing visions to transform those around you.

Complete these sentences:

"While out in the world, these are the three most important things I learned about my feelings . . ."

"With my journey over, I see these patterns in how I live my life . . ."

"Based on what I found on my journey, this is how I intend to live my life differently from now on . . ."

We enter the garden as the sun is waning.

We sit in the shade and, after a time, we begin to drift into a blissful slumber.

The sky reddens around the furrows left by the fleeing sun chariot. Still we sleep on, oblivious to the gentle lapping of the fountain, the sudden appearance of a cricket and a nightingale.

And now before us looms the angel of the journey, mute, its great wings barely moving in the evening breeze.

In the dream, we will greet this noble and powerful being. We have met before. Its quiet invitation to undertake a new journey will both excite us and inspire us.

We will be transfixed.

In the dazzling light from the angel's face, we will have forgotten the pleasant comforts of this kingdom—for we are beckoned to new kingdoms, even finer and more radiant than this.

Travel On

You have completed your journey. Now you see that the arc comes full circle back to the beginning.

You have transformed yourself into a conscious traveler. By making your trip an archetypal journey, you have elevated it to a high spiritual plane.

The way of the traveler is to see, hear, feel, and assimilate every experience in the enchanted process of the journey.

You are the protagonist of your drama, the hero of your quest. You have been abroad on a mission, and it has been an expedition to reach the spiritual heart of yourself—there to be transformed.

Travel in the outer world is a metaphor for the epic journey inward. And the reward for this sacred sojourn is the spiritual gift of grace: the grace of peace, the grace of self-knowledge, the grace of wisdom.

The Tao Te Ching says, "You can see the whole world without leaving your room. You can see the universe without even looking out your window. By looking inside oneself, the wise person sees with the heart and the mind, and the heart and the mind see everywhere."

Now you are listening for the call of a new journey. When it comes, you will be ready.

You create a new travel shrine.

It is empty at the moment, awaiting the promise of a new journey.

The journey within has made me wiser and more powerful. Transformed, I wait in silence, in strength. Soon the gods of travel will call me forth again. And I will heed the call.

Continuing the Journey

*I thought of a labyrinth of labyrinths, of one sinuous spreading
labyrinth that would encompass the past and the future and
in some way involve the stars.*

Jorge Luis Borges, *The Garden of Forking Paths*

Walking the Labyrinth

Travel as spiritual practice is the meaning of the labyrinth, the ancient walking map that looks, from above, like an unfolding flower.

Until a few years ago, the labyrinth was virtually unknown to our culture as a tool for meditation and contemplation. The labyrinths at famous medieval cathedrals, such as the one at Chartres outside Paris, had fallen into disuse and disrepair. Labyrinth designs on coins, tapestries, and illuminated manuscripts piqued the interest of art historians, but the connection between the concentric circular path and the metaphor for an inner journey of the spirit appeared to be lost.

Recently, along with many other ancient spiritual practices, the labyrinth has been rediscovered. Now the beautiful rosette design is appearing in churches, retreat houses, yoga and meditation centers, and even in the backyards of private homes. Portable labyrinths painted on canvas or oilcloth are available for individuals or groups in workshop settings. Bookstores sell miniature labyrinths that you can trace with your fingertips.

When I first encountered the labyrinth many years ago on a trip to England, I seemed to know instinctively what it was and how I was to use it. I removed my shoes, stepped onto the path, and immediately went into a contemplative state. The rush of emotions I felt and the peace I experienced during that first walk made me seek out other labyrinths. I found them in France and Italy and Germany. Now I am learning that there are labyrinths in many different configurations all over Europe and, in fact, all over the world— and that they have been in continual use for more than four thousand years.

The labyrinth walk is a metaphor for the journey of life. The path is a winding one, full of surprises, twists, and turns. Your path runs parallel to the paths of others walking the same road. You encounter others who appear to be walking alongside you at one moment and in the next are far away.

At the center of the labyrinth is a resting place. You reach it after a meandering journey that takes you close to the heart of it all, then back out again suddenly, and then finally to the core. You stand there and feel what it is like to be at the center of the center of yourself. Standing here in this symbolic "within" of yourself, many feelings may arise—doubt, uncertainty, even fears, or serenity, compassion, wholeness . . . a peculiar human emptiness that is also filled with a divine presence.

When you are ready, you begin the journey out—back to the "real world." Again you encounter people walking in opposite directions, sometimes practically rubbing elbows with you. But no one collides; each is on a separate sacred path.

At the end of the path, which is also the beginning, you feel a sense of completion. It is as if you have lived your entire lifetime in those concentric circles and serpentine lanes.

A fundamental difference exists between a labyrinth and a maze. A maze is meant to trick you; it wants you to figure your way out of it with your brain. The labyrinth is just the opposite; it is a walk you do with your heart. It has no blind alleys, no hidden passageways. It is simply the walk of life. You need to make the decision to enter the labyrinth, but once on it, the path is inexorable to the center of your being.

As an archetype for the sacred journey of life, the labyrinth has no equal in spiritual practice.

Walking it with an open mind and an open heart will bring marvelous insights about who you are, where you have been, and where you are going. The way of the labyrinth is the way of the traveler on life's seemingly inscrutable and unpredictable journey. Like the most sacred of life's undertakings, the labyrinth asks only for the courage to begin walking it and then the willingness to surrender.

Once you make that commitment, the path itself does the powerful work of ever-ascending personal transformation.

I never travel without my diary. One should always
have something sensational to read in the train.

Oscar Wilde, *The Importance of Being Earnest*

Recommended Reading

Throughout this book I have referred to classic works of travel literature by quoting passages from them. Here is a brief list of some of those books and a few others that I believe will support your interest in the spiritual aspects of travel.

Artress, Lauren. *Walking a Sacred Path: Rediscovering the Labyrinth As a Spiritual Tool.* New York: Riverhead Books, 1996. the Reverend Artress, who is both a psychotherapist and a priest, rediscovered the labyrinth for modern readers and spiritual seekers. Her description of how she recovered walking the labyrinth as a spiritual practice is stirring, and her practical suggestions for using it in one's daily life are priceless.

Barrett, Bill. *Brown Water Café.* Santa Fe, NM: Owlseeall Publishing, 1998. A cross-country trip provides the setting for Barrett's reflections on our culture. This is a personal travel journal with a strong philosophical and spiritual thrust. Compare with *What Really Matters,* by Tony Schwartz, which is also an account of a trek across the United States in search of spiritual values and meaning and, one's place in world. A wonderful example of an outer journey turned inward by the author's insightful reflections.

Campbell, Joseph. *The Hero with a Thousand Faces*. Princeton, N.J.: Princeton University Press, 1990. A classic, originally written by Campbell in 1949, about how the myths of the world inspire and enrich our lives. Along with several other books by Campbell, this seminal masterpiece influenced many other scholarly and popular works, including Hollywood's *Star Wars* films and their imitators. Campbell's books can seem difficult reading at times, but they are well worth the effort.

Carlson, Richard and Benjamin Shield, eds. *Handbook for the Soul*. Boston: Little, Brown, 1995. Essays about how to nourish the soul by, among others, Lynn Andrews, Wayne Dyer, Robert Fulghum, Ram Dass, Jack Canfield, Stephen Covey, John Gray, Marianne Williamson, Sydney Banks, Thomas Moore, and Bernie Siegel. Helpful for seekers looking for practical spirituality in today's world. A wide assortment of spiritual choices, with the same underlying theme, from the leading voices in the spiritual self-help field.

de Saint Exupéry, Antoine. *Wind, Sand, and Stars*. New York: Harcourt Brace, 1967. For this master of lyrical writing, flight is a metaphor and a symbol of human aspiration. One of the great books on travel—and life—it imparts a sense of sacred movement to all the stages of the journey. If you have never read it, you are in for a tremendous treat.

Durrell, Lawrence. *Bitter Lemons*. New York: Marlowe & Co., 1996. Although he is best known for the four novels that comprise his Alexandria Quartet, Lawrence Durrell is an insightful and accomplished writer on travel. *Bitter Lemons,* set in Cyprus, is one of his three island books, which also include *Prospero's Cell* (about Corfu), and *Reflections on a Marine Venus* (about Rhodes). You can virtually smell the scent of the sea in these books.

Dyer, Wayne. *Your Sacred Self.* New York: HarperCollins Publishers, 1996. These reflections on the spiritual core at the heart of human nature suggest that approaching life as a sacred event will enhance everything we do. Dyer's reflections here, and in his other books, have helped many modern spiritual seekers. Eminently practical and quite moving.

Graves, Robert. *Greek Myths*. Baltimore: Penguin, 1993. A classic reference book on mythology by the author of *I Claudius, Greek Myths* is for both the serious scholar and the casual inquirer. Graves looks at all the myths and their dramatis personae to form a compendium of Greek thought and religion.

Hamilton, Edith. *Mythology.* New York: Back Bay Books, 1998. You might have encountered this book in grade school and high school, and

again in college. Look at it again for its wisdom about the human
condition and its astonishingly good storytelling. A world-renowned,
popularly written collection of myths, carefully organized, mostly
from the ancient Greek and Roman traditions. An engrossing and
entertaining read.

Housden, Roger. *Sacred Journeys in a Modern World.* New York: Simon &
Schuster, 1998. An inspiring travelogue and spiritual journal. Widely
published British author Housden speaks about how to bring spirituality
into our everyday lives, which he sees as spiritual journeys. His writing
is insightful and helpful, often embroidered with comic asides.

Klein, Eric. *Sacred Journey.* Blue Hill, ME: Medicine Bear Publishers, 1998.
Seeker Eric Klein writes about the nature of the spiritual path and about
his own spiritual unfolding. The theme of these channeled messages
from the masters is ascension—the evolution of the human species into
higher realms of spirituality. The book includes messages from Mother
Mary, St. Germain, Sananda, and other masters of the spirit from the
other side. No ordinary journey, this. But the open-minded can find
here some fascinating descriptions of the human condition in the
process of change.

Kornfield, Jack. *A Path with Heart.* New York: Bantam Doubleday Dell,
1993. Western Buddhist master Kornfield speaks about his personal,

practical wisdom, based on twenty-five years of practicing and teaching the path of awakening. Kornfield sees life as a spiritual path to be followed with courage, grace, and wisdom. Through this and other books, he has helped to bring a new interest in Buddhist thought and practice to the West.

Lawrence, D. H. *D. H. Lawrence and Italy: Twilight in Italy, Sea and Sardinia, Etruscan Places*. Baltimore: Penguin, 1997. For Lawrence, known mostly for his fiction, all travel tends to be inner travel. An eerie feeling pervades these books, which are magnificently written and meticulously observed, because much of what Lawrence writes about has changed in the nearly hundred years since he visited Italy. But, the industrialization of the modern world aside, his insights about the human situation are brilliant, and his travel descriptions are delicious.

Morris, Mary. *Nothing to Declare*. New York: St. Martin's Press, 1999. This 1988 travel memoir is filled with brilliant insights into both Latin America and travel in general. The continent has not changed appreciably since Morris wrote it. Her travel commentary has a freshness to it, and she makes wise observations about her experiences.

O'Reilly, Sean, James O'Reilly, and Tim O'Reilly, eds. *The Road Within: True Stories of Life on the Road*. San Francisco: Traveler's Tales, Inc., 1997.

Writers, among them Annie Dillard, Huston Smith, and Natalie Goldberg, speak of travel as an inner journey. This is one of those books that you can read in bits and pieces. It's valuable for the insights of its authors and its overall theme of understanding journeys we take in the outside world as metaphors for inner searches.

Raine, Kathleen. *India Seen Afar.* New York: G. Braziller, 1991. The third volume of Kathleen Raine's autobiography, in which she reflects on the "India of the Imagination, the term of every spiritual quest." This is a journal of a homecoming, as the author returns to India and sees it—and herself—anew. Wonderful writing, especially in her descriptions of the colorful and mysterious sides of India.

Schwartz, Tony. *What Really Matters.* New York: Bantam, 1996. A journalist writes about his travels in search of learning what really matters in life. During a personal pilgrimage across America, he comes into contact with a vast array of New Age approaches to spirituality. A marvelous, informative read—and now, a time-capsule report on the state of the spiritual self-help movement in the 1990s.

Thesiger, Wilfred. *Arabian Sands.* New York: Viking Press, 1985. Sir Wilfred Thesiger's moving description of his journeys through the Arabian Peninsula. There is no better book, I think, that confirms the distinction between a tourist and a traveler. Sir Wilfred is a traveler who sets out to educate himself about the Bedu of Southern Arabia, tribes of people nearly extinct. This book not only serves to educate about a small fraction of the Arab population of the Middle East, but also about the glories of travel and discovery.

Vega, Janine P. *Tracking the Serpent: Journeys to Four Continents*. San Francisco: City Lights Books, 1997. Poet Janine Pommy Vega searches for truth and self-realization in the far corners of the world. Particularly good as a woman's unique view of what can be discovered about oneself "out there," far from home.

Williamson, Marianne. *A Return to Love*. New York: HarperCollins, 1993. The internationally acclaimed author speaks on the rewards of bringing a spiritual dimension to our lives. Her material is based upon and is her personal reflection on the spiritual book, *A Course in Miracles*. Williamson has become one of the major leaders and spokespersons in the renewal of spiritual interest in the United States.

Wurlitzer, Rudolph. *Hard Travel to Sacred Places*. Boston: Shambhala Publications, 1994. A well-known novelist and screenwriter makes a life-changing journey through Southeast Asia: Cambodia, Thailand, and Burma. An outstanding example of how travel can effect personal transformation in a heart open to the possibility of change. The exotic landscape Wurlitzer travels supports his inner discoveries.

Yogananda, Paramahansa. *Autobiography of a Yogi*. Los Angeles, CA: Self
    Realization Fellowship, 1997. Originally published in 1946, this
    account of one man's spiritual journey is one of the great classics of
    spiritual literature. Yogananda was in the vanguard of those who
    brought Eastern philosophy and spirituality to the West. In this
    remarkable memoir, he speaks about living saints, prayer, meditation
    (highly practical), and the ultimate meaning of life. An anchor book for
    a spiritual library.

The use of traveling is to regulate imagination by reality, and instead of thinking how things may be, to see them as they are.

Samuel Johnson

Websites of Interest

One of the best ways to enhance your appreciation for travel as spiritual practice is to check in from time to time on some websites. They will give you up-to-date information on travel to sacred sites, pilgrimages, guided retreats, workshops, seminars, and conferences, and suggest other interesting ways to expand your knowledge and heighten your awareness.

I have found the websites below quite helpful. I encourage you to take a look at them. Since sites change frequently, you can also perform a search for "travel and spiritual" or "inner journeys," and come up with dozens of other informative sites.

InfoHub.com Specialty Travel Guide
www.infohub.com
A web portal that presents a wealth of material on travel in general—and, if you type in "spirituality" or "pilgrimage," yields excellent current information on travel that can support your spiritual aspirations.

The Dreamtime
www.thedreamtime.com

This site offers information on a wide variety of spiritual self-help topics,
  including alternative healing, astrology, tarot (a serious presentation),
  the I Ching, and other modalities for self-awareness. Under
  "spirituality," type in "travel."

WOW Institute
www.wowinstitute.org

A spirituality site for and about women that has a thorough and highly
  informative travel section. It's even possible for women to network for
  travel with other women who share similar interests. The site presents
  a tremendous amount of good material, and it is always current.

Beliefnet
www.beliefnet.com

Beliefnet.com went into operation as the new millennium began. It is a
  richly informative site that has set the standard for pertinent and
  well-written materials—and it's as up-to-date as the morning
  newspaper. The travel section is an excellent resource. Also see the
  sections on personal spirituality, which give a context for traveling
  with a spiritual purpose.

Awakenings
www.lessons4living.com/labyrinth.htm
This is one of the best of the many websites devoted to the labyrinth. It
offers links to other interesting labyrinth sites and presents an excellent
history and survey of the subject. The graphics, showing the many
different configurations of the labyrinth, are particularly helpful.

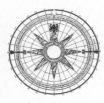

The feeling remains that God is on the journey, too.

Teresa of Avila

Acknowledgments

For their assistance in clarifying and augmenting the material for this second edition, I would like to thank my colleagues at LifePath Retreats, Dr. Beverly Nelson, Deidrea Johnson, and Michael Herbert. And at Avalon Travel, Donna Galassi, Mary Beth Pugh, and my editor, Rebecca Browning.

For their helpful advice and encouragement, I would also like to thank Snow Anderson, Lynn Andrews, Judi Baumbach, Reid Callanan and the staff at the Santa Fe Photography Workshops, Chris Calloway, Barbara Neighbors Deal, Dianna Delling, Diane DiRoberto, Monica Faulkner, Allison Feliciano, David Christian Hamblin, Georgelle Hirliman, White Jade, Annie Jennings, Hal Isen, Krandall Kraus, Margaret Olsen and Pancho Kohner, Mike and Saliann Kriegsman, Michael Peter Langevin and the staff at *Magical Blend* magazine, Sabine Lucas, Bill O'Donnell, Paul O'Donnell and the staff at Beliefnet.com, Stephanie and Sebastian Puente, Ron Savarese, Robert Owens Scott and the staff at *Spirituality and Health* magazine, Tamar Stieber, Deborah and Leo Tallarico and the staff at *Spiritual Renaissance* magazine, Lupita Tovar, Skye Wentworth, and Rosemary Zibert.

©Diane DiRoberto

About the Author

Joseph Dispenza has studied spirituality firsthand, living eight years as a monk—one of those years in total silence. He is the author of twelve other books and numerous articles on a variety of topics, including holistic healing, cinema, travel, and personal spirituality.

For several years, he headed the education division of the American Film Institute and lectured in communication at American University in Washington, D.C. Later, he established a successful film school at The College of Santa Fe in New Mexico and taught courses in media ethics. He also served as the founding director of Parcells Center for Personal Transformation in Santa Fe, an institute that advances the philosophy of holistic healing.

Joseph is the co-founder of LifePath Retreats in San Miguel de Allende, Mexico, which offers guided retreats of self-discovery, based on the mythic journey as presented in this book, for people seeking lifepath clarity.

Joseph welcomes correspondence from readers. You can email him at Joseph@LifePathRetreats.com, or visit the website www.LifePathRetreats.com.